WHAT IS EDUCATION?

WHAT IS
EDUCATION?

Philip W. Jackson

THE UNIVERSITY OF CHICAGO PRESS

Chicago & London

KH

PHILIP W. JACKSON is the David Lee Shillinglaw Distinguished Service Professor Emeritus in the Departments of Education and Psychology and in the College at the University of Chicago. He is the author of several books, including *Life in Classrooms*, *The Practice of Teaching*, and *John Dewey and the Philosopher's Task*.

The University of Chicago Press, Chicago 60637
The University of Chicago Press, Ltd., London
© 2012 by Philip W. Jackson
All rights reserved. Published 2012.
Printed in the United States of America

21 20 19 18 17 16 15 14 13 12   1 2 3 4 5

ISBN-13: 978-0-226-38938-7 (cloth)
ISBN-10: 0-226-38938-3 (cloth)

Library of Congress Cataloging-in-Publication Data

Jackson, Philip W. (Philip Wesley), 1928–
    What is education? / Philip W. Jackson.
        p.   cm.
    Includes bibliographical references and index.
    ISBN-13: 978-0-226-38938-7 (hardcover : alk. paper)
    ISBN-10: 0-226-38938-3 (hardcover : alk. paper)
1. Education—Philosophy. 2. Education—Aims and objectives.   I. Title.
    LB14.7.J33   2012
    370.1—dc22

                                    2011007976

♾ This paper meets the requirements of ANSI/NISO z39.48-1992 (Permanence of Paper).

11/26/12

For Jo

Einstein:

"The conceptual basis of physics
is a free invention of the human mind."

Me:

"As goes physics,
likewise education."

Contents

Acknowledgments

The seed responsible for the ultimate flowering of this book was planted while I was a student at the New Jersey State Teachers College in Glassboro (now Rowan University). It was there that I was first introduced to the educational writings of John Dewey. I am grateful to the officials of that institution for awarding me a tuition scholarship that made it possible for me to attend. Without that aid I likely would never have gone to college. I am also grateful to my many fine teachers there, far too many to name in full, I am pleased to say. One of them, Leonard Mancuso, gave me his own hardbound copy of Dewey's *The Public and Its Problems* when I graduated. I treasure the memory of that generous gift and remain its proud owner to this day.

I also am deeply indebted to the faculty and staff of Teachers College, Columbia University, where I again received a tuition scholarship that allowed me to complete my graduate studies. There too I encountered several faculty members who not only had studied Dewey's writings but had known him. Their memories of Dewey and their indebtedness to his ideas helped make him a living presence in my life. Arthur T. Jersild, Harold Rugg, and Bruce Raup in particular contributed much to my budding interest not only in Dewey but in philosophical matters in general.

It was not until I joined the faculty of the University of Chicago, however, that my interest in Dewey really blossomed. When I arrived there in 1955 the university's Department of Education had several faculty members who were particularly interested in Dewey's work. They included, most notably, Harold Dunkel, Robert McCall, and Joseph Schwab. Dewey's bust was proudly displayed in the Education Library, which was then in Judd Hall. The university's Laboratory School, adjacent to Judd, stood as a vast brick-and-mortar monument to Dewey's philosophical foresight and a physical reminder of his enduring contribution to American education. In that environment a serious study of Dewey's vast oeuvre became almost mandatory. For years I engaged in that study, conducting seminars on several of Dewey's major works and encouraging graduate students to move in the same direction. I even, for a time, served as director of his widely acclaimed Laboratory School. I am grateful indeed to the university for the intellectual climate it provided and for the opportunity to undertake all those efforts.

Among the many students who attended those graduate seminars, several have since become close friends, and we continue to keep in touch. I have profitably discussed with each of them many of the notions contained in this book. Former students who have aided me in this way include especially Rene Arcilla, Robert Boostrom, Craig Cunningham, Maureen Donne, Mary Driscoll, David Granger, David Hansen, and the late Lauren Sosniack. I am deeply grateful for their loyal support and encouragement.

Catie Bell, another of my former students, now a close friend and currently a teacher of English at the university's Lab School, deserves special thanks. She not only helped nurse me back to health after a serious illness, which sets her apart from all but professional caregivers and family members, she also has been a faithful walking companion for the past several years. Three mornings a week, almost without fail, the two of us stroll along a route of a mile or more from my house to the shores of Lake Michigan and back. On many days lately the walk has also included a welcome stop at a nearby coffee shop. During those long hours of walking and chatting Catie and I have discussed every aspect of this book many times over. I have gained beyond measure from those exchanges.

I thank Elizabeth Branch Dyson, my editor at the University of Chicago Press, for her strong support and encouragement. I also thank the three anonymous reviewers selected by the press. Their careful reading and thoughtful suggestions helped to eliminate several errors and greatly strengthened the manuscript. For those weaknesses that remain, I accept full responsibility.

Finally, this book is dedicated most sincerely to my dear wife. I owe her the greatest thanks possible for her steadfast companionship and loving support over the years.

Introduction

What is there to learn about education that we don't already know? That question has one obvious answer: as educators we must learn to do whatever we do professionally better than we've done it to date. That straightforward answer points emphatically in an empirical direction: at one level it calls for more experimentation and research.

There is clearly much merit in that call. We surely do need to continue experimenting with practices and policies, large and small, seeking to improve on what we already know how to do moderately well. But is that all? Just continue to experiment empirically? Based on what one reads these days in the newspaper and also in a fair number of educational journals, the answer appears to be yes. A pragmatic spirit, bent on discovering "What works!" clearly dominates much of educational thought from classrooms to boardrooms, from policy think tanks to administrative offices.

But there's another answer. It posits that we need to learn not just how to improve on current practices but also how to *think* differently about education. We need to approach it afresh from time to time, to look at it from a new angle. This calls for reexamining many of our old ways of thinking, calling into question matters that we perhaps haven't bothered to consider for quite some time. In short, we need to *rethink* education from the ground up.

1

"Rethink education? Look at it afresh? What good will that do?" the skeptic asks. A truthful answer can only be, "We don't know." We can't know what good it will do until we've done it. That is so, moreover, by definition. New ways of thinking about education have unpredictable outcomes just because they are new. They may or may not translate into improved practices, either slowly or quickly. They may in fact do little more than reaffirm the soundness of many of our *old* ways of doing things. We may wind up right where we started. In fact, we're almost bound to do so, at least in part.

But even that lack of progress, should it happen, constitutes an advance. If all we do is refurbish many of our convictions, bringing them up to date, so to speak, by aligning them with other changes in our current ways of thinking, we at least will have done that. Even if their substance doesn't alter, freshly examined thoughts cannot help but leave us more firmly convinced, and a firmer conviction should always be welcomed. It is certainly not to be breezily dismissed; it may be fully as beneficial to our overall well-being as a spanking new idea.

Let's assume, then, at least at the start, that there may be some obvious merit, psychologically speaking, in trying to rethink education from the ground up. "Fair enough," the skeptic might reluctantly concede, "But how do you do that? Where do you begin?" In a sense, all that follows may be looked on as offering an answer to that question—a single, very tentative, and quite idiosyncratic answer. It traces my own effort to blaze such a path, with scant experience in such matters and with very little outside guidance save reading what others have said and trying to benefit from their words. I presume that many who join me in taking up the challenge will find themselves in a very similar position.

To reveal where that path led in my case is to run far ahead of the story, yet one or two preliminary generalizations set the stage for what follows. A couple of rules of thumb have served me well and might serve others who try to follow a similar path. Because of their generality I can safely divulge them here without giving away too much.

The first rule is to start with something you believe to be un-equivocally true about education and gradually build on that, simply by musing on where such a belief takes you. At the same time you should anticipate that that initial truth, no matter what it is, will have to be modified—made more truthful or less untruthful, whichever seems preferable. The comedienne Penn Jillette is said to have quipped, "One of the quickest ways to find out if you're wrong is to state what you believe."[1] Another way of putting it might be to echo Hegel, who was fond of observing that *a* truth seldom if ever turns out to be the *whole* truth. Patient reflection on almost any partial truth soon makes that clear.

That firm starting place is more or less the strategy I adopted in writing this book. I began by assuming that everyone already knows what education truly is, so I couldn't figure out why Dewey was asking a long-ago audience of listeners and later his readers to think once again about a question whose answer was so obvious. I soon discovered that there was much more to education's truth than I had ever considered, more than I had even begun to imagine.

The second rule is this: prepare for a round trip. That second expectation, incidentally, is simply a variant of the first rule, turned on its head. Another way of putting it might be, expect to wind up sooner or later where you started. Indeed, déjà vu is almost bound to occur several times in the course of your thinking, because thought has a way of circling back on itself. It spins, one might say, on its axis.

The first line of T. S. Eliot's "East Coker," part of his *Four Quartets*, reads, "In my beginning is my end." The last line of the same poem declares, "In my end is my beginning." The poetic truth contained in those contrasting lines is familiar to anyone who has tried to think deeply about anything. Poets, at least the best of them, are especially aware of that ancient truth. Beginnings and endings, starts and finishes, belong together. They seek to be conjoined.

Perhaps those two methodological points offer enough hint of what is to come to get us under way. What follows from taking that hint seriously awaits imminent disclosure.

1. As reported in the *New York Times*, June 11, 2010, C25.

1

Dewey's
Parting Words

My writing this book was initially spurred by remarks John Dewey made before an audience of educators in 1938 at the close of a series of lectures sponsored by Kappa Delta Pi, an honorary educational society, and later published in a volume titled *Experience and Education*.

I have used frequently in what precedes the words "progressive" and "new" education. I do not wish to close, however, without recording my firm belief that the fundamental issue is not of new versus old education nor of progressive against traditional education but a question of what anything whatever must be to be worthy of the name *education*. I am not, I hope and believe, in favor of any ends or any methods simply because the name progressive may be applied to them. The basic question concerns the nature of education with no qualifying adjectives prefixed. What we want and need is education pure and simple, and we shall make surer and faster progress when we devote ourselves to finding out just what education is and what conditions have to be satisfied in order that education may be a reality and not a name or a slogan. It is for this reason alone that I have emphasized the need for a sound philosophy of experience.[1]

1. John Dewey, *Experience and Education* (1938; New York: Collier Books, 1963), 96.

4

Those words puzzled me when I first read them, in the late 1940s or early 1950s, as I recall, a decade or so after *Experience and Education* was published. I was preparing to be a middle school teacher and had only recently learned that John Dewey was not the inventor of the Dewey decimal system. Why would the Dewey of educational fame end his book by asking his readers to devote themselves "to finding out just what education is"? Most of them were probably professional educators already, I reasoned, or like me were on the way to becoming so. Surely, even neophytes already knew the answer to that question. I certainly did! Why, then, urge them to rethink it? Indeed, the more I pondered Dewey's advice, the stranger it seemed.

It was not just the general request that troubled me. The way Dewey worded his advice was equally puzzling. He threw out not one but several questions for his audience to ponder, and some seemed downright baffling. The adjectives "pure and simple," for example, sounded odd applied to the noun "education." I couldn't figure out what those qualifiers meant. Was Dewey suggesting that if we put our minds to it we would ultimately arrive at the one *true* conception of education, the one every clear thinker would be virtually *forced* to accept?

That possibility struck me as improbable to say the least. If there were a single, true conception of education, I reasoned, it certainly would have been discovered ages ago. Surely by now, after centuries of educational thought and practice, any innermost secrets of education ought to have come to light. Moreover, wasn't that precisely what Dewey was presenting with such obvious enthusiasm throughout the pages of *Experience and Education*? Wasn't it at the heart of what he called "a sound philosophy of experience"? Also, wasn't he contradicting himself by making it clear through the sheer magnitude of his own effort, not just in that book but in lots of his other writings, that a true understanding of education was anything but pure and simple?

I had read very little philosophy when I first began puzzling over Dewey's words, but the little I had read led me to suspect that he was inviting his readers to think about education *philosophically*, the

way Socrates might have done. The trouble was, at the time I didn't
know where to go with that thought. I have since read a fair amount
of philosophy and come to a better understanding of what Dewey
was asking his readers to do. Oddly enough, I have also come to believe that Dewey himself may not have been fully aware of exactly
what he was asking. In fact, I'm sure he couldn't have been.

What Dewey was up to with his parting advice is something I've
mulled over for quite some time. In fact, my search for an answer
has occupied me almost constantly for years. That search has taken
me on a much longer and more arduous journey than I ever dreamed
of at the start. It has led, above all, to an in-depth reading of both
Kant and Hegel, along with the writings of several of their illustri-
ous contemporaries.

I concentrated on those two writers from the start not only because of their obvious prominence as philosophers but also because
I knew that early in his career Dewey had been deeply influenced by
neo-Hegelian thought. I also knew he remained indebted to Hegel
even after that influence waned. I thought, therefore, that a close
reading of one or two of Hegel's major works might hold the key to
a better understanding of what Dewey was asking his 1938 audience
to do. I had no idea at the time that the decision would lead to a
prolonged study of both Hegel and Kant and that I would wind up
becoming a more ardent Hegelian than Dewey himself was during
most of his long career. More important, however, as the result of
that study I ultimately came to think about education in ways that
were new to me. I trust that some of what I learned might interest
others—my chief reason for writing this book, which presents some
of the highlights of my own journey and invites others to join me in
reliving them.

TAKING DEWEY AT HIS WORD

The mere mention of my benefiting from reading Kant and Hegel
runs far ahead of the story. Long before I turned to Hegel and his
contemporaries for guidance, I first had to decide whether to take
Dewey at his word, which not everyone I asked was willing to do.

When, for example, I confided to a friend who shares my long-standing admiration for Dewey that I intended to spend some time trying to figure out what the old boy was getting at in that final paragraph of *Experience and Education*, his reaction was quick and to the point. "It sounds to me," he said with a laugh, "as though our revered mentor, Big John, was just looking for an easy way to close his lecture. I'd bet he wasn't thinking very deeply at all about what he was saying at that point."

Of course I'd considered that possibility and had rejected it long before talking to my friend. I had done so for two reasons. First, I felt it would have been totally out of character for Dewey to conclude a series of lectures by taking an easy way out. That just wasn't his way of doing things, or so my reading of a fair number of his public lectures had led me to believe. He was far more likely to remain the patient expositor to the bitter end, even if he had to be a bit long-winded.

Second, I felt the thrust of Dewey's final paragraph was at least understandable, even if other things about it remained a bit puzzling. What he was asking his audience to do—think deeply about the meaning of education—was quite in keeping with what one might expect given Dewey's academic credentials. Philosophers through the ages have made it their business to prod others into thinking more deeply than they otherwise might about a host of familiar concepts—courage, love, and virtue, to name just a few. Dewey, it seems, was just living up to that age-old expectation. He was behaving as philosophers have done for centuries. That was reason enough, I concluded, to take him at his word.

In any event, I finally decided that the best way to judge the worth of Dewey's advice was to try following it for a time and see where it led. What follows constitutes a crude recounting of that journey, with a few explanatory asides along the way.

DEWEY'S FOUR QUESTIONS

One of the first things I struggled with was what to make of the four questions Dewey invited his 1938 audience to consider.

1. What must anything whatever be to be worthy of the name education?
2. What is the nature of education with no qualifying adjectives prefixed?
3. What is education pure and simple?
4. What conditions have to be satisfied so that education may be a reality and not a name or a slogan?

What chiefly puzzled me about those questions was their sheer number. Why so many? Did Dewey think of them as truly separate, or were they variants of a single question that he kept rewording for some reason? The first three sounded repetitious to me, though the fourth stood apart. I invite you to reexamine the four as listed to see if that assessment seems right.

But if the first three are all variants of a single question, what, we might ask, is its invariant form? Could it simply be, What is education, period? That possibility came to mind because of the way Dewey presented his questions. He ran them together hastily, as though it really didn't matter which of them individual members of his audience might choose to address. "Take your pick," his mode of presentation seems to imply; "one question is as good as any of the others to start with."

But I soon concluded that that reading of his intention was itself a bit too quick. For when I tried to picture how Dewey might respond to such a proposal, I imagined him saying, "No, no. The question is not 'What is education, period.' That's far too unadorned a query. What I would like educators to think about is what education is *really and truly*. What is it *fundamentally, essentially, absolutely*? What is it in some final sense, *when all the chips are down*, let's say, or *when all is said and done*?" My conjuring of his impatience did not stop there. I pictured him going on with his explication more or less as follows: "Another way of putting it would be to ask about education's basic worth as a human endeavor. What makes it so crucial to our well-being as humans? Why should professional educators, or anyone else, for that matter, devote their lives to its pursuit?"

My imagination, I slowly began to realize, was taking me toward expressing the tacit moral urgency I sensed lay just below the surface of Dewey's closing advice. Was I wrong about that, I wondered? Was Dewey really seized by moral urgency in posing his questions? Did he want his audience to feel that urgency? Possibly, I concluded. But to nail that conclusion down would take a lot more work. Or so it seemed at the time.

SEARCHING FOR A SHORT ANSWER

I had begun my investigation thinking that Dewey was asking his audience to come up with something like a concise definition of education, perhaps one that might be easily committed to memory and even one whose truth was blatantly self-evident.

That possibility had the backing of common sense. People usually seek concise definitions when they look up a word or a concept in a dictionary. They want something brief, just enough to fill a temporary gap in their knowledge. With that accomplished, they can turn back to whatever they were doing.

I came close to taking that route myself, but instead of turning to a dictionary for help as one normally does in such circumstances, I decided the definition Dewey was calling for was not something I could look up. It had to be original. It had to be what *I* thought, not what someone else thought or what a dictionary said. In short, it had to be exclusively personal, yet also public in the sense of being shareable. Why else would he address his four questions to his audience as a whole? He clearly wanted them each to strike out on their own in search of an answer. All of that was related to what I took to be the moral urgency of his questions.

Acting on that assumption, I took a stab at my own answers to Dewey's set of questions without seeking outside help. After a few minutes' thought, I came up with this short definition: *Education is a socially facilitated process of cultural transmission.* Its brevity appealed to me. In fact, I was rather proud of it. "Only nine words in all. Not bad," I thought.

The trouble with that nine-word definition, I soon realized, was that it was too brief. In attempting to say everything in the fewest possible words, it said almost nothing. It also sounded rather pompous. Yes, education was and is and perhaps always will be a socially facilitated process of cultural transmission. But as a friend I shared my brainchild of a definition with was quick to remark, almost with a sneer, "Yeah, yeah, sure it is. But education's a lot more than that." I had to agree, of course, but *what* "more" than I had said? What had my definition left out?

Well, for one thing, as I quickly came to see, my nine words contained no explicit recognition of moral purpose, surely an important part of what education is all about, as I had already recognized. It also did not distinguish education from other activities that involve socially facilitated cultural transmission. Consider what happens when a tourist asks a stranger for directions. A word or two and a finger pointing this way or that is all the situation requires. Surely we wouldn't call that brief exchange education, would we? "Of course not," I suspect most of us would say. But why not? It certainly is an instance of socially facilitated cultural transmission. What does our hesitation to call it education say about the answer to Dewey's questions?

Another problem I had to acknowledge is that my short answer failed to address Dewey's fourth question, which asks what conditions have to be met to make education a reality rather than just a word or a slogan. But how can one address that question? What does it mean to make something a reality rather than just a word? It obviously means to *do* something rather than just *think* about it. But what is the connection between thinking and doing? It was at about this point that my budding interest in Hegel, based at the time on little more than a cursory reading of his *Phenomenology of Spirit*, began to yield dividends.

HEGEL'S ABSTRACT AND CONCRETE UNIVERSALS

Hegel distinguishes between abstract universals and concrete universals. Abstract universals are concepts that have been almost entirely stripped of content. They stand above particularization, existing in the mind alone. My nine-word definition of education comes close to being such an abstraction.

Concrete universals are also cognitive objects. but they are more fully determined than abstract universals. They thus come closer to being realized (concretely identified).

This distinction, crude as it is, helps us understand better what Dewey may have been getting at with his four questions. The first three seem to be aimed at seeing education as an abstract universal, in the loftiest terms possible, as I tried to do with my nine-word definition. The fourth question, however, asks us to consider what conditions have to be satisfied so education may be, as Dewey puts it, "a reality and not a name or a slogan." This clearly invites us to view education more concretely—that is, as a concrete universal.

But the order in which Dewey places that final question is itself suggestive. It implies that the concrete universal cannot be raised before we have framed the concept more abstractly. It is as though Dewey were saying, "Think about the concept in a grand manner before you get down to brass tacks."

That sounds like good advice, whether or not Dewey meant his questions to be read that way, but can it be followed? Can we think about education grandly and abstractly before we have come to know it concretely? That's more or less what I tried to do with my nine-word definition, but as we have seen, the result was unsatisfactory. Moreover, I couldn't have come up even with that unsatisfying result if I hadn't already known a lot about education in very concrete terms. I must, then, have been moving backward, sorting through all I already knew about education and tossing out everything but its most abstract formulation. This would contradict the suggestion implied in the order of Dewey's four questions. Which is it, then? Are we to begin our thinking *abstractly* or *concretely*?

I believe Hegel would say that when seeking to generalize we have no choice but to start with a positive affirmation that aims at universality and see where it leads. What we usually find, however, often in short order, is that the statement we began with is deficient in some way, as happened with my nine-word definition of education. That opening gambit, if the word is allowed, will likely contain a bit of the truth but certainly not its totality. It will need to be qualified or elaborated on in some way. Conversely, it may turn out to be partially or even totally false, needing correction or erasure.

The cognitive exercise Dewey recommends moves us, at least initially, toward ever greater abstraction. He wants us to think of education as ideally conceived—as God might will it to be, let's say. Yet he also wants us to think of it realistically, as something that could possibly be accomplished rather than an idle fancy. This means that to accommodate both requirements, our thinking needs to oscillate along that posited abstract/concrete continuum.

Another advantageous way of conceptualizing that continuum is to think of its abstract extreme as referring to what is essential and its concrete extreme as referring to what actually exists. This gives us *essence* at one extreme and *existence* at the other. Substituting these two terms for the more conventional labels *abstract* and *concrete* prompts us to see that the essential and the existent have a way of intermingling that calls for persistent thought and diligence to discern their separate contributions to our understanding. Even then, we can seldom if ever be absolutely certain we've made the distinction correctly. For the essential can never be *seen* to exist in the way physical objects are seen. It can only be posited by thought itself, which means it awaits verbal expression.

Here a further example may help. If we walk into a school, what do we see? We see a lot that can be precisely described by everyone who speaks the same language. We see classrooms, students, and teachers. We see desks, textbooks, and chalkboards, and a host of other physical objects. We see what people are doing and we hear what they are saying. All of those objects and activities may be said to exist. What we don't see are the purposes they serve, which we may readily assume will turn out to be multiple. We have to infer or be told what those purposes are. Do those purposes also exist? Yes and no. They do so by analogy. We routinely say things like, "Now I *see* why you are doing that," even though we don't really see anything tangible.

CONTINGENT AND IMMANENT TRUTHS

At this point another of Hegel's notions comes in handy. He draws a sharp distinction between contingent and immanent truths. Contingent truths refer to conditions that could be otherwise. Immanent truths refer to conditions that must be; they lie buried, as it were, deep within the entity under consideration. They constitute its essence. When the entity is an organic being, its immanent truth is genetically established. That genetic endowment determines the genotype—the dogness of the dog, the roseness of the rose. When the entity is a human activity, such as education, its immanent truth, which consists of its highest purpose, is normatively established. It is historically achieved. Expressed in these terms, Dewey was inviting his audience to ponder the immanent truth of education, to distinguish it from those conditions that may characterize a lot that goes on in today's classrooms but that, on close inspection, turns out to be contingent rather than immanent.

But how is that accomplished? How does one distinguish between contingent and immanent truths? Certainly not solely by a single visual inspection, or even repeated inspections. To move from an understanding of the way things are to an understanding of the way they should be calls for something more than an empirical investigation. It calls for moving beyond experience itself and entering a realm some would call transcendental or even metaphysical. It is the realm of what ought to be rather than what is. Its primary elements consist of "goods" that are thought to apply universally. They thus are offered as truths to be accepted unconditionally or absolutely.

It was at about this point in my own exploration of following Dewey's 1938 advice that I was struck by the notion that "the pursuit of truth" might be a far better way of summarizing the task of education than "the pursuit of knowledge," which is far more commonly used as shorthand for what education is all about. I was led to that thought principally by my reading of both Kant and Hegel. Their combined theories helped me realize that there are several kinds of truth beyond those that Hegel calls "contingent" and "immanent." Truth, I came to see, is a bit like Jell-O. It comes in different colors and flavors. Moreover, I came to realize that education as a human endeavor is deeply implicated in the pursuit of all those kinds of truth—so much so, in fact, that the task of teachers facing a roomful of living students could well be described as *trafficking in truth*.

2

Trafficking in Truth

KINDS OF TRUTH

Leaving aside for a time the question of education's highest truth—what Dewey seems to be urging his audience to think about and a concept I shall ultimately return to—five kinds of truth seem central to education's mission. I've tentatively labeled them *factual*, *systematic*, *instrumental*, *moral*, and *subjective*. I'm not too happy with those labels. As they stand, they're far too much of a grab bag. But let's make do with them for the time being and see where they lead.

The important point is that none of these five kinds of truth is watertight. Treated as containers, they all have leaks that constantly allow their contents to seep out and mix. That seepage is one of the generic conditions that keep teachers on their toes. They must continually determine the chief kind of truth that's on the table at the moment.

Also, I must be clear on what I'm claiming about these kinds of truth. Not at all am I suggesting that these are the only kinds of truth. I only contend that each has a place in any complete picture of the workings of education. Each, I claim, is therefore at least worthy of mention. With that caveat firmly established, I will offer a brief description of each type before turning to how they fit within the give-and-take of classroom life.

Factual Truths

Factual truths are the smallest—truth's pennies. People call them facts. They provide the kind of information that often can be communicated in a flash and readily verified by the senses. Though capable of standing alone, they frequently come bundled for ease of access, like the entries in a telephone directory or items on a list. In Dickens's *Hard Times* the teacher Mr. Gradgrind, comically portrayed if fundamentally cruel, celebrated the primacy of facts as educational content. "Facts, facts, facts, children!" he cried.

Systematic Truths

Systematic truths are in the form of complex structures whose elements cohere, held together by myriad strands of logical and inferential reasoning. They constitute "bodies" of knowledge. They might be likened to pieces of fabric or to an intricately patterned carpet or appliqué. The titles given to standard school subjects, such as English or chemistry, are convenient labels for such systems of thought. I call them "systematic," but they could also be called "ideational," following Kant's use of the term "idea," which he borrowed from Plato. They represent clusters of notions associated with particular concepts. If the chief job of factual truths within an educational setting may be said to be providing desired information, that of ideational truth may be said to be enlightenment, a far more ambitious undertaking.

Systematic truths are open-ended. Our grasp of them is always finite, but it remains capable of expansion, even infinitely so. In a sense, then, even though they are objects of thought and therefore products of the human spirit, systematic truths are like living organisms. They develop. They grow. They can also wither and die. At times they die through sheer disuse, like a native language that is no longer spoken.

Some would say the chief business of education is preserving and transmitting systematic truths. That is more or less what I was thinking when I used "cultural transmission" in my nine-word definition of education. That popular assumption has considerable validity, yet it also misses a lot. It depicts the task of education as far more cut-and-dried than it is. It fails to convey the dynamic aspect of "trafficking in truth" that my taxonomy intimates.

Instrumental Truths

Instrumental truths are methodologically sound. They are about how to do things. They show the way and outline the steps to be taken. They have more to do with physical action than with thought alone, so their contents tends to be practical rather than theoretical. They focus on technique. In written form, they provide the kind of advice found in cookbooks or in the handbook of rules for playing a game. As live performances, they demonstrate how something should be done.

Moral Truths

Moral truths are truths about how to live one's life. They cover our relationship with ourselves, our fellow humans, and other living things. They usually are posited in very general terms, often as maxims that can be easily remembered and readily brought to mind. The Bible's Ten Commandments and the Golden Rule stand as paradigms.

From an educational perspective, moral truths are so basic to the well-being of a human community, are instilled at such an early age, and are so broadly applicable that most educators tacitly assume knowledge of them, at least in broad terms, almost from the start. In short, they are largely taken for granted. This means they are often overlooked except when breached.

An important exception occurs in the earliest grades, particularly nursery school and kindergarten, where we often find young children being explicitly instructed in rudimentary forms of common courtesy and social manners, which are fundamentally moral. They likewise are brought to the fore in organizations explicitly dedicated to one or another form of moral education, or "character training." Think, for example, of what goes on in scouting programs and religious schools. There too, as in the earliest years of schooling, moral truths are certainly far from overlooked. Nonetheless, those exceptions do not seriously alter the basic claim that moral truths tend to be largely ignored in most public and private school classrooms. Whether that should cause concern remains to be addressed. I shall treat the question when I return, as promised, to an examination of education's highest purpose.

Subjective Truths
We come now to a category of truth that has very special significance for educators. What makes subjective truths distinctive in educational terms is their personalized status. They are what individuals *take* to be true about themselves, about others, and about the world in general. They include everything that holds true *for* that person regardless of what others may think or believe. Though personally held, they may be publicly acknowledged as well, accepted as true by others. But that need not be the case universally. Some subjective truths, such as superstitions, may be looked on as false by the world at large.

What makes these truths especially important for educators is that in cognitive terms they constitute education's bottom line. They are what teachers consciously seek to establish or modify. For in the end, the goal of teaching is not simply to communicate knowledge to those lacking it. (That was one of the drawbacks of relying so heavily on the word "transmission" in my nine-word definition of education.) Rather, the teacher's goal is to have her students *possess* whatever knowledge she transmits. She wants them to accept it as their very own. It then becomes true for them *subjectively*.

Taking ownership of knowledge does not occur automatically, as most teachers know. It involves more than simply hearing something said or being shown how something works. It requires following with understanding what is said or shown by someone else, assenting to its truth as it becomes known. It also requires remembering what was tacitly accepted and being able to reproduce it in sufficient detail when conditions call for its retrieval. The latter requirement presumably justifies the widespread practice of giving examinations in schools and colleges. Testing, of course, involves a risk—it subtly, if not blatantly at times, conveys distrust of those being tested.

TRAFFICKING IN TRUTH AS EDUCATION'S MISSION

What has our brief inventory of these five types of truth revealed? What does it say in answer to the questions Dewey posed so long ago? To me its value lies principally in the recognition that, though education may traffic in truths of all kinds, its chief task is to bring those truths to life. It must make them accessible, interesting, and perhaps even vital to those at the receiving end of that transaction. This means, most of all, transforming truths that fit within the first four categories into truths of the fifth category, those I have labeled subjective. Doing so is no small task, as I have tried to make clear. Every teacher knows that without being told.

At this point I must interject a thought that is definitely out of sequence but too germane to withhold. I apologize for the digression.

Toward the end of my circuitous search for the key to what Dewey was asking his audience of educators to do, I came to the conclusion that he was inviting them to undertake the impossible. He was asking for a finite answer to an infinite question. He wanted each of his listeners to launch into the task of delineating the essence of education, presumably in its totality. But that totality has no limits—its conditions are unbounded. Its status as an object of thought is what Kant would call *transcendental*. It lies outside experience.

Yet that a transcendental object cannot be experienced does not make it unworthy of contemplation. It can still serve as a signpost giving direction to thought. Kant puts it like this:

> Although we have to say of the transcendental concepts of reason: *They are only ideas*, we will by no means regard them as superfluous and nugatory. For even if no object can be determined through them, they can still in a fundamental and unnoticed way, serve the understanding as a canon for its extended and self-consistent use,

through which it cognizes no more objects than it would cognize
through its concepts, yet in this cognition it will be guided better
and further.[1]

Thus, in keeping with Kant's observation, Dewey was inviting his
listeners to think long and hard about what is absolutely essential to
both the theory and the practice of education. He did not bother to
warn them that they had no chance of arriving at any final answer.
And that's probably just as well, for some might have balked at setting off on such a futile undertaking. But as the urgency of his words
made clear, he knew that the only hope of enduring educational
progress is having individual teachers and school administrators labor mightily to achieve the impossible, guided in some "fundamental and unnoticed way," as Kant puts it, by the idea of a truth whose
totality may lie beyond experience but that can clearly be attained in
at least a fragmented and preliminary way.

The question that keeps recurring is whether the guidance im-
plicit in the concept of education can be made more explicit. Can
we move from education as a mere word or slogan, as Dewey might
say, or as a transcendental signpost, as Kant might prefer, to something far more helpful? I believe we can, and I'm sure Dewey and
Kant would agree. Indeed, I tried to accomplish this on my own near
the start of this essay. But despite the initial glow of pride my nine-
word definition occasioned, that early effort turned out to be only
momentarily satisfying. My emergent conviction that education has
more to do with the pursuit of truth than with the transmission of
knowledge and that subjective truth, as I now call it, was of primary
concern to educators was yet another move in that same direction
and, I would say, more heuristically fruitful to boot. The image of
teachers almost literally "trafficking in truth" is one I continue to
find compelling. I trust that a fair number of you now fully agree.

In classrooms across the land, public and private truths perpetually jostle for the upper hand in an exchange as old as education it-

---

1. Immanuel Kant, *Critique of Pure Reason*, ed. Paul Guyer and Allen W. Wood
(Cambridge: Cambridge University Press, 1998), 403, A329.

self. The powers of "I" and "we" lock horns over whose truth shall reign, and the contest is on: first person singular against first person plural, winner take all. Plural is the usual victor, as we know, and well it should be, for maintaining a human community depends on that outcome. But its victory does not take place without overcoming a fair amount of resistance now and again, and sometimes not without leaving first person singular significantly worse off for having undergone the exchange.

All teachers share what they know with their students. They want them to adopt the thoughts of others. But if they have given the matter sufficient thought, as most teachers have, they also want their students to think independently, to be personally convinced of the truth of what is being taught.

How do you win that conviction? In a host of ways, of course, but principally by allowing for objection and dissent as instruction proceeds. For the teacher, this means tolerating interruptions, entertaining unexpected questions, taking note of puzzled facial expressions, and doing whatever it takes to quell doubts as they arise. All of that interplay contributes to the meaning of trafficking in truth.

In classrooms, managing that traffic is chiefly the teacher's responsibility. Teachers structure the classroom activity by selecting the material to be studied, assigning seatwork or homework, lecturing, leading discussions, and so on. In doing so they largely determine the type of truth that has prominence at any given moment. But that control is only external; at least ideally, the same thing goes on internally during periods of self-instruction. Objection and dissent then take place without being openly voiced. Control of truth's traffic passes to the individual, where it belongs in a free society. Its final manager, under the best of conditions, turns out to be none other than thought itself, thought doing its own thing, exercising its freedom, turning on its axis, realizing its potential.

3

Preconditions of Education

In terms of education, the crucial point contained in the last sentence of chapter 2 is summarized in the phrase "under the best of conditions." That parenthetical remark serves as a warning that the best of conditions need not always hold. Thought may be naturally inclined to exercise its freedom, but it typically must be patiently trained to do so. That training is a large part of education's task. Left to itself, thought often falls short of realizing its capability.

What conditions prompt the development of thought? How does education help to establish them? It does so principally, as we know, by settling on a limited set of cognitive objectives in the form of course content and then doing its best to keep students' attention on that content long enough to yield preestablished levels of insight and understanding. That process is so well known that it calls for little explication.

What is not so obvious are some of the preconditions that undergird that familiar process, increasing the likelihood of success. The prefix *pre* emphasizes both their logical and their temporal status. They are "pre" in that they precede, both logically and temporally, the establishment of the physical conditions that teachers and students consciously experience. They thus tend to be overlooked. Better said, they escape our attention. Yet that does not mean they are inoperative as principles. They still are acted upon, albeit almost unconsciously. Once we become aware of them, it's useful to think about them when making educational plans or designing specific instructional strategies.

How many such preconditions are there? To be frank, I have no idea, but let's begin with three. Although they are fundamentally an outgrowth of my reading in philosophy, they should be readily understood by educational practitioners, for they owe as much to my observation of teachers in action and to my own experience as a teacher as to anything I've read. *Motion, ground*, and *rationality* are the terms I'll use to introduce them. They deal with the way thought *moves*, with how it is *grounded*, and with the primacy of its adherence to the rules of *rationality*.

THOUGHT IN MOTION

Thought is always on the move. It seldom if ever stands still. Such is its nature. Yet, as every teacher knows (and every other human as well), the movement of thought is not always as we or others would like it to be. Thought sometimes drifts. It wanders. It flits from one subject to another like a butterfly moving from flower to flower or a bird hopping from one branch to a higher or lower one. Thought even loses its way from time to time. It sometimes resists moving the way others want it to move and may react to attempts at direction in a belligerent, angry way.

One of the main tasks of education is channeling thought's movement—retaining its focus, keeping it on the right track, as one might say. That task is by no means readily accomplished, as every teacher knows. It takes work, sometimes hard work, and the greatest effort may be futile.

What does the expression "on track" mean when applied to thought? Is there a single track it typically runs on? Or might there be more than one?

Based on what philosophers tell us, plus what I have observed, I conclude that thought, when disciplined, moves predominantly along three tracks. Graphically portrayed, it moves either *horizontally*, *vertically*, or *elliptically*.

As we witness its motion in classrooms, we often see it switch direction, jumping from one track to another, sometimes in seconds. Those switches are not always easy to detect from the outside, nor are they always consciously understood. They may be signaled by muttered single words or short phrases that escape notice.

Horizontal Thought

Thought moves horizontally as it seeks to extend its province by adding incrementally to what is already known or what has just been said. This lateral extension is by far the most common move undertaken in ordinary educational discourse, such as in a lecture or a textbook exposition or even a free-floating discussion or conversation.

Tiny words like "also," "and," "moreover," "furthermore," "next," "additionally" serve as the logical hinges that link parallel thoughts, marking the gradual extension of their domain. As teachers or even as independent learners, it helps to become sensitive to those small marks of thought pushing itself forward. That horizontal movement prompts us to speak of knowledge as an organic entity that increases in size over time. We thus speak of it as *growing*.

Vertical Thought

Thought moves vertically in search of the universal, the essential, the ultimate, seeking to rise above itself or, conversely, to penetrate downward until it reaches bedrock. It aims for the highest or the most fundamental level of generalization possible, even to transcending the limits of experience and becoming purely symbolic or figurative.

That movement in the direction of self-transcendence can also be portrayed, as I just said, as a move not skyward but in the opposite direction, reaching down rather than up. Either way, it is seeking a kind of closure, the final word on a subject, the point beyond which there is nothing left to say. "Most important," "basically," "fundamentally," "ultimately," "finally," "this above all" are words and phrases we commonly use as we approach the terminus of that vertical movement.

Kant applied the terms "intensional" and "extensional" to mark the vertical/horizontal distinction. For him, the horizontal movement of thought, the extensional, was synthetic in its function. It brought many things together to form a composite picture, an aggregation. The vertical movement, the intensional, was analytic. It sought the deep distinctions of the concept and was chiefly the business of philosophy and metaphysics. Here's the way Kant put it in his *Logic*:

> With the synthesis of every new concept in the aggregation of coordinate characteristics the *extensive* or *complex* distinctness is increased; with the further analysis of concepts in the series of subordinate characteristics the *intensive* or *deep distinctness* is increased. The latter kind of distinctness, as it necessarily serves the *thoroughness* and *conclusiveness* of cognition, is therefore mainly the business of philosophy and is carried farthest especially in metaphysical investigations.[1]

As a pair of terms, *complexity* and *depth* sum up the distinction Kant is making far more succinctly, I would say, than his explanatory paragraph does. *Coordinate* and *subordinate* do almost as well. Horizontal movement increases the coordinate characteristics; vertical movement ascends or descends in the series of characteristics that are arranged hierarchically like the rungs of a ladder.

Elliptical Thought
Thought's elliptical movement serves to qualify or correct assertions that have been made. It turns thought back on itself the way a planet orbits the sun in an elliptical arc. Its outward motion posits a claim. Its return motion tempers what has been said in some essential way. "However," "but," "yet," "nonetheless," "on the contrary" are pivotal words and phrases that signal the turning point of thought's qualifying motion.

---

1. Immanuel Kant, *Logic* (New York: Dover, 1974), 65.

This form of thought's motion receives its fullest treatment in the writings of Hegel. He treats the concept of negation as a driving force, a tiny engine pushing thought along. He argues that the essence of reason is to seek the truth. But the truths it hits upon are not the whole truth, merely partial, because truth and falsity are bipolarities, inexorably coupled. One cannot exist without the other. Every truth therefore comes tainted with some kind of nontruth in the form of something about itself that awaits revision and correction. Since its deficiency is often not immediately evident, repair entails turning back on itself.

So there we have the three major tracks along which education seeks to channel thought. It seeks, in short, to broaden and deepen thought's grasp of the truth while ridding it of error and other shortcomings. It also seeks to harness thought's motion, to prevent it from wandering off and wasting its energy on daydreams and other fruitless projects.

THE GROUNDING OF EDUCATIONAL EFFORT

How does a teaching session get under way? It often begins, as we know, when the teacher announces its subject matter or anticipated content in very general terms. "This is World History 101," the history teacher says as she strides into class on the first day and writes the course title on the board. "Today we're going to begin to explore quadratic equations," the math teacher intones on a Tuesday morning. "Now, children, let's listen to a really exciting story," the nursery school teacher says with delight as she addresses her flock of three- and four-year-olds.

Those introductory statements establish a baseline for the course as a whole or for the day's activities. They announce what's going to happen. They're like chapter titles or subheadings in a document, a verbal promise. Metaphorically, they constitute bedrock. Everything that follows builds on them or issues from them as from some overarching plan.

Yet the foundation such statements seek to establish is seldom as secure as it might appear. It may serve a useful purpose, true enough, but bedrock it is not. Its status remains problematic no matter how firmly declared. This is chiefly because it often is set by the teacher alone or in concert with other educational authorities without seeking or receiving the students' consent.

This state of affairs is so well known that it hardly bears mention. Yet it is crucial to understanding at least one of the characteristic dilemmas that teachers and students jointly face. Let's take a closer look at why.

The teacher who announces the course title on the first day of class is doing more than making sure everyone is in the right classroom and is attentive and ready to go. She is also doing more than simply making an announcement. She is suggesting that what is about to take place is important, something she believes in and thinks is worth sharing. The same is doubtless true of the math teacher and the nursery school teacher. The actions of all three convey resolute conviction.

It is likely that many, if not most, of the students present share that conviction, but not the way the teacher does. They look forward to being taught whatever the teacher promises to teach them.

Many students surely do willingly accept the teacher's intention and eagerly await its unfolding. But not everyone present necessarily does so. Some may be far less convinced about the worth of what is to come. The difficulty most commonly occurs when education is compulsory or, at a more refined level, when specific courses are "required" rather than "elective." Under such conditions a sizable number of students may remain unconvinced of the ultimate worth of what is being taught. They may also question their own capacity to understand the material. These may drop out or, if they stay on, turn into the classroom laggards that so concern the conscientious teacher.

Indeed, even as they announce what the course as a whole is to be about or what topic they are going to treat next, teachers may be nagged by doubts about the true value of what is to come. They may wonder whether this is the way to teach this or that or even whether it is worth teaching. When such doubts emerge we once again face, in a far more serious form, the distinction between public and private truths. Teachers who question the value of what is being taught are in a far more precarious position than are students who harbor similar doubts. If the ground teachers stand on turns out to be quicksand or ankle-deep mud, the whole enterprise is threatened.

The crucial point with respect to the grounding condition is that effective education rests on a conviction, shared by all present, that the material being studied is of considerable value. If only the teacher holds that conviction, she faces an arduous task. If most of her students agree but a significant number do not, the task is still challenging. But when the teacher herself remains unconvinced of the value of what she is doing, the odds in favor of her success tip dangerously toward the negative.

Does that mean the teacher must be cocksure about every single thing she plans to do? Must her intentions always be solidly grounded? Of course not. Teaching is a risky business. Missteps and unfortunate decisions are bound to occur. The person who is afraid of facing those risks definitely shouldn't be a teacher.

At the same time, all teachers have the responsibility of trying to make single lessons or even a whole course of study cohere in some intelligible way. They must show how things hang together. That effort most commonly entails calling attention to what is essential about what they have just taught or are about to teach. The trouble is, however, that all such moves are basically judgmental. What is declared important or essential always remains open to challenge. People can disagree.

This means there is no bottom line to the grounding condition. The ground teaching rests on is seldom as solid as the teacher might like. Doubts emerge. Misgivings are aired. Claims must be defended. Reasons must be given and arguments constructed for things the teacher may see as self-evident. Considering the need for such exchanges brings us about as close as we can get to the ultimate mission of education—extending rationality.

THE PRIMACY OF RATIONALITY IN EDUCATION

The claim that rationality has primacy in educational affairs is of course little more than a truism. Everyone knows education chiefly concerns becoming increasingly rational. That's basically why people pursue it. Yet that truism cloaks a fair number of complexities. Let's look at a few of them.

The initial phase of becoming more rational begins informally at home and is continually expanded by our informal dealings with people and objects in the world at large. Over time such casual experiences contribute to the development of what most people would call common sense.

Common sense is of course essential to everyone's physical and psychological well-being. Without it we would be less than human. Those who lack rudimentary common sense must be protected and cared for by others. Yet acquiring common sense alone is far from enough to make humans fully rational. In fact, when too heavily relied on, common sense has distinct disadvantages as a cognitive strategy. Formal education is explicitly designed to address some of those disadvantages and, if possible, remedy them.

The Shortcomings of Common Sense

The greatest drawback of common sense is that, as its name implies, it relies too heavily on the senses. It tends to stick almost exclusively with what is immediately seen and heard. It also tends to be hasty in its judgments, which alone can become a severe handicap. Haste, as we know, not only makes waste, it blocks contemplative thought.

To conjure common sense developing in action, picture a mother interacting with her young infant. "Where's your nose?" she asks while repeatedly guiding the child's finger to his nose, and soon he begins to point correctly on his own. "See the birdie!" she says, pointing to a picture of a bird, and the child echoes the name he hears. She continues such patter as she turns the pages of the picture book, and before long the child can name a host of common objects. That vignette provides a classic instance of how common sense comes into being. Human rationality rests on a host of such building blocks lovingly established.

The chief difficulty with such learning is that it remains rudimentary at best. Naming objects is surely an important achievement;

there's no denying its significance. But there's a lot more to being able to think than naming objects. Such an exercise is too cut-and-dried. It judges assertively rather than tentatively or questioningly. It doesn't launch inquiry; rather, it puts an end to further investigation. Once something is named, it stands ready to be shelved and put away. ("And whatsoever Adam called every living creature, that was the name thereof" [Genesis 2:19]. Thus ends, therefore, that phase of the story.)

There's a lot to be said for the person whose judgments are commonsensical and down-to-earth. It's good to have such people around. But formal education has the explicit task of moving beyond common sense.

Kant's Treatment of Understanding and Reason
In his *Critique of Pure Reason* Immanuel Kant draws an important distinction between understanding and reason, clarifying the limitations of common sense. Understanding, Kant points out, is essentially unitary and judgmental. In its simplest form, as we have just seen, it involves placing an identifiable object within a broader category that subsumes it. The mother who points to a picture of a bird and says "bird" is helping her child understand the world in the most rudimentary fashion.

Reason makes use of such judgments, naturally enough, but it lifts them up a notch, or even several notches, by linking them syllogistically to form complex inferential structures. The building and repair of those structures constitute the chief business of formal education.

Those structures that reason constructs are designed to house thoughts, the way physical edifices are built to serve a variety of purposes. Some grow incrementally like soaring cathedrals; others remain simple like huts. They go by many names. The more elaborate ones are often called theories or arguments; the simpler ones, theses or explanations or even just excuses or alibis. All are forms of reason whose artful construction goes beyond common sense and must be learned through diligence and effort.

From Reason to Speculative Thought

The move from common sense to reason, as Kant defines it, constitutes a genuine advance in the extension of rationality. But that move does not bring us to the limits of reason. Those limits become clearer in the writings of Hegel, who attempts to push beyond Kant's conception. He calls his proposed advance a move from reason to speculative thought. Its basic form is dialectical.

The essential difference between Hegel's speculative thought and Kant's reason boils down to this: speculative thought tends to be inclusive, whereas reason tends to be exclusive. That's far too simplistic a formulation, to be sure, but it contains enough truth to merit our attention.

The inclusiveness of speculative thought allows it to embrace and ultimately resolve its own negation. It acknowledges and even welcomes the inexorable coupling of true and false, yes and no, being and not-being. As thought becomes increasingly speculative, the conjunction of "both/and" largely replaces reason's disjunctive "either/or."

The move from a purely argumentive mode of thought to a more speculative one takes on special significance within an educational setting, because it allows teachers to adopt a strategy that has become a mainstay of enlightened pedagogy in a democratic society. That strategy, in a nutshell, consists of soliciting responses to direct questions or encouraging spontaneous contributions to a teacher-led discussion and then shifting the focus on each response from approval to disapproval. It calls for being both *appreciative* and *critical*, switching from one to the other in a twinkling.

The teacher responding in a speculative mode says things like, "That's a very good point, Sarah, but have you considered . . ." or "I certainly agree with you, Fred, but I wonder . . ." or "Wow. I would never have thought of that myself, Mark. Good for you! But would you say . . ." Each such response from the teacher is intended to be supportive and encouraging while clearly signaling the limits of every attempt to reach the truth in some final sense.

I recently discussed this strategy with a seasoned high-school English teacher, who quickly pointed out that the real goal of a well-led discussion, at least in high school, is to encourage students to adopt an approach like the teacher's when responding to each other's contributions. Each student then builds on what a fellow student has said, in a way that communicates respect. As students catch on to the benefits of responding that way, the teacher reports, they come to do it automatically.

The Role of Negation in Speculative Thought

The teacher's combination of appreciation and criticism when responding speculatively calls attention to an aspect of teaching fraught with danger: offering criticism. Criticism entails negating at least some aspect of what the student has said or done. It is absolutely necessary to pedagogy, yet it can cause harm, as every teacher knows. Hegel's treatment of the role of negation in advancing thought seems instructive and may be helpful to teachers as they consider both the necessity and the danger of criticism.

Hegel insists that thought moves forward chiefly by partially negating (or denying) its apparent accomplishments. This not only involves coming to see that more remains to be said on a particular subject, it often includes a frank and sometimes painful recognition that at least some of what has already been said or thought is downright wrong and needs correction.

But negation is not something that happens just now and again. It goes on continually, with no limits. What replaces something deemed incorrect will in time also turn out to be imperfect, and it too will have to be replaced or negated. Hegel calls this inevitable progression "the negation of negation." It happens all the time.

The impulse that triggers this sequence resides within thought itself. It does not originate externally. The internal nature of its origin causes Hegel to describe thought as having the capacity to determine itself. What brings about that self-determination in the realm of thought is the revelation of a contradiction that had escaped notice. In Hegel's own words, "contradiction is the root of all movement and vitality; it is only in so far as something has a contradiction within it that it moves, has an urge and activity."[2]

The prospect of continually confronting contradiction and being forced to revise our thoughts may sound a bit disheartening when stated so bluntly. And it certainly can be so from time to time. In his preface to the *Phenomenology of Spirit*, Hegel calls the route thought takes as it moves forward on its own power "the way of despair."[3]

Fortunately, the situation is not as bleak as it might appear. Despite intermittent discouragement, the possibility and even likelihood of genuine progress remains. This is because overcoming contradiction as Hegel portrays it is constructive as well as destructive. It does not entail the total rejection of what has gone before. Though it partially cancels previous thinking, it leaves room for preserving part of the advance. It preserves past accomplishment but raises the ante, moving thought to a higher level of discourse.

In German this tripartite movement of canceling, preserving, and elevating thought finds expression in the noun *Aufhebung* and the verb *aufheben*. Unfortunately, English contains no exact equivalent of either term. Anglophone translators of Hegel and of other German writers who use those familiar terms have resorted to using "sublation" and "sublate," English words that are so rare they do not even appear in the *Oxford American Dictionary*.

The essential point, however, is that for Hegel negation does not result in the rejection of the thinking that has preceded it. It is only a single step in the three-beat oompah-pah waltz of thought. Moreover, if we look closely at the dynamics of *Aufhebung* as Hegel uses it, I believe we can see a clear resemblance to the familiar pedagogical strategy of appreciation followed by criticism that I described.

As has just been said, that strategy calls for handling a student's erroneous or malformed statement tactfully: correcting or

2. Georg W. F. Hegel, *Science of Logic*, trans. A. V. Miller (Amherst, NY: Humanities Press, 1969), 439.

3. Georg W. F. Hegel, *Phenomenology of Spirit*, trans. A. V. Miller (Oxford: Oxford University Press, 1977), 49.

strengthening it, but in a way that does not embarrass the student and even builds constructively on her initial effort. "Well, not quite, Sarah, but you have a good point," the teacher might say, "Now let's see how it might be improved." Cancel. Preserve. Elevate. The three steps of *Aufhebung* could hardly be more clearly implied.

There is of course an important difference between what a sensitive teacher does in such a situation and what thought does quite on its own, which is to say, what it would do if afforded sufficient freedom. In the situation described, the teacher's motivation is clearly divided. She obviously wants to avoid embarrassing her student, but she just as clearly wants to penetrate to the truth of the matter at hand. Thus she soft-pedals the *cancel* phase of the Aufhebung move, almost making it seem that the student has said something quite worthwhile. Then she artfully builds on the remark, hoping to raise the level of understanding not just for that student but for the whole class.

When we go through a similar experience on our own, self-consciously undertaking the three steps of *Aufhebung*, the soft-pedaling that the teacher adopts becomes unnecessary. Thought instinctively confronts its imperfections in private, without risk of public embarrassment. For the most part the solitary thinker greets her own imperfections and corrections rather stoically, although she may sometimes feel chagrined at taking so long to detect a shortcoming of her own making. Also, if she has already spoken out, she may be uncomfortable at needing to take back what she said. Such feelings aside, however, thought turning on its own axis—as it does when conditions are right, Hegel insists—does not normally cause unease. Instead, as the persistent thinker comes to discover, thought's unceasing restlessness can yield the deepest pleasure. One of the chief goals of education is to have that insight emerge. The question is, How does that happen?

Thought as Its Own Reward
As I have already suggested, most teachers try to make classroom life as pleasant as possible by overlooking their students' weaknesses while applauding their efforts. This means reacting far more

positively than negatively to almost everything students say and do, saying yes far more frequently than no.

It is easiest to follow that positive strategy at the very earliest stages of learning. It is perhaps exemplified most dramatically in the reception teachers and parents give to the earliest drawings or paintings of very young children. We commonly find them prominently exhibited in classrooms and proudly displayed on refrigerator doors at home. Even the public at large finds their crudeness so charming that commercial artists sometimes imitate it in advertisements.

Avoiding criticism becomes more problematic with older students, though even with adults courtesy probably makes teachers react positively more than negatively. Few teachers enjoy being a thorn in a student's side.

Yet critical negation from teachers and from school authorities in general remains essential to education. Letter grades and the widespread use of various paper-and-pencil tests testify that such criticism is ubiquitous and perhaps necessary. It hovers like a dark cloud over most exchanges between teachers and students from the earliest grades forward. Students stand in the dock with their teacher as judge. There's no getting around it.

Yet, as I have pointed out, there are ways to soften the teacher's judgment, including "soft-pedaling" the critical step of the *Aufhebung* strategy (the initial move of canceling) while emphasizing its more constructive steps of preserving and elevating.

Another way of handling the negation criticism entails and reducing its sting is to help the student become his own critic. This might well be called "the Socratic solution," since it resembles the strategy Socrates employed in his spirited dialogues with his interlocutors. In those celebrated exchanges he typically aimed to have his more persistent questioners slowly become aware of the flaws in their own assertions. He seldom directly pronounced his combatants wrong. He didn't have to. They delivered their own verdicts.

The trouble with the Socratic solution is that it usually takes a fair amount of time. It's not easy for a student to develop an awareness of the weakness in his own thinking all on his own. It customarily calls for nimble thinking by the teacher who is trying to prompt that awareness. Socrates's artful use of probing questions stands as the prime example of what it takes to do that job.

Yet another strategy for promoting self-criticism is to require students to write down their thoughts and then carefully edit their own work. For lack of a better term, let's call this the write-revise solution. Of course it can be used only with students who are mature enough to undertake such a task, but its value as an aid to clear thinking remains indisputable. What makes it work is the distance it creates between what one *had* thought and what one *now* thinks. That temporal gap, no matter how small, allows for the emergence of a "second thought," making possible a change of mind.

Are those rudimentary observations too obvious to bear mention? Possibly so. I'm certainly willing to believe they might be. But classroom discussions and writing assignments are often handled so fast that I suspect not nearly enough time is usually given for thought to become as self-determining as Hegel insists it is inclined to do. Slowing down instruction may, paradoxically, allow thought more room to move at its own pace and thus in the long run speed its progress.

Yet time alone is ineffective as a causal agent, for not everyone's thoughts remain bent on self-improvement and self-determination no matter how much nature may incline them in that direction. Thus, beyond time to think, many people need patient cultivation of that natural tendency, and that is what the schools are uniquely designed to provide. People need *time* to think, but they also need be encouraged to make good *use* of that time. They need to be exposed to models of rational excellence. They need be praised for their own efforts at self-improvement and cheered along as they progress. They need ample opportunity to practice such efforts at minimal risk to their self-esteem. In short, they need a nurturing environment in which to make the negation of their own thoughts a habitual step toward better thinking.

Thinking and Feeling
I have something else to say about the combination of praise and criticism that teachers are continually called on to dispense: feeling

and thinking never occur separately. They invariably go hand in hand. Thinking always involves feeling and feeling always requires thought, even if only to attach a name to it, as in "I feel angry" or "I feel sad."

That connection between thought and feeling may be almost too plain to mention, yet recognizing its truth brings to the fore something that makes teaching distinctive. Though they clearly do their share of thinking, teachers who confront their students face to face are not just thinkers. Far from it. They think and feel in the presence of others, and they must intend to be helpful to those in their care. Thus they must constantly remain keenly aware of how those others—their students—think and feel.

An important aspect of that awareness is recognizing that thought is always creative. Its products, even when modest, connote the emergence of something new. Each one signals a personal flash of cognitive achievement. Thus, someone who ventures to express a thought in class likely feels some satisfaction, if not downright pride or pleasure. Herein lies the ultimate justification for the teacher's initially responding appreciatively, perhaps even overly so, to a student's comment. Textbook authors, public lecturers, or others who "teach at a distance" don't have to deal with the immediate reactions, spontaneous or solicited, of those they address as do those who teach under more conventional conditions.

4   Unifying Essence and Existence

In his *Systematic Theology* the Protestant theologian Paul Tillich makes much of the distinction between essence and existence, a distinction we've already been introduced to. In part this is a way of distinguishing the work of the theologian from that of the philosopher. Most of the great philosophers of the Western world, Tillich insists, have been principally interested in revealing essences. They have sought to uncover the structure of Being in itself. The interests of theologians, however, at least the kind Tillich sought to be and to promulgate in his writings, go beyond a concern with the structure of Being. They are chiefly interested in what it *means* to be, what facing today's existential challenges means on a personal level. Phrased formulaically, the chief task of the theologian, Tillich asserts, is to provide theological answers to existential questions.

What are theological answers? They are answers that seek to be definitive in some absolute or unconditional sense. Such answers, at least as Tillich understands them, derive in large measure from one or another of the world's religious traditions. They are final rather than contingent. They are where the explanatory buck stops.

And what are existential questions? They are questions that encompass the totality of existence as humanly experienced. Fully embraced by those who sense their urgency, they are of ultimate concern.

When existential questions and theological answers are properly aligned, the theologian's argument goes, the unity of essence and existence is momentarily attained, at least in a fragmentary and preliminary way. In sum, as the *essence* of any entity—its destined form or shape—becomes more fully known, its *existence*, in all its manifestations, takes on additional meaning.

It may seem a stretch to turn to a theologian for help in understanding what Dewey, the secular philosopher par excellence, was asking his audience to do back in 1938. And so it is, in a way. But Dewey and Tillich were contemporaries throughout the first half of the twentieth century, and both were dedicated teachers. Most important of all, both were advocates of a distinctly human kind of striving. That striving typically takes the form of a search for final answers to questions that have no final answers, though we often feel as though they do. Kant would call such questions *transcendental* rather than *empirical*. They are what draws Tillich and Dewey together, even though their take on such matters also separates them fundamentally. So, though closing the breach between theologian and philosopher may require a stretch of the imagination, it is not nearly as challenging as it may seem at first.

Dewey invites his audience (later his readers) to continue to ponder the essence of education. That advice is timely and well taken. The urgency of doing so is also clearly implied in the pileup of questions that Dewey uses to lure his audience into accepting his challenge. But he fails to make clear just what such an effort entails. He ends by emphasizing the need for a sound philosophy of experience, yet he does not bother to point out that the essence of education cannot be directly experienced. It cannot be divulged empirically; it can only be inferred. That process of inferring is where the relation between essence and existence comes in.

As it exists today and has existed in the past—which is to say, as directly experienced and as revealed in descriptive accounts of its history—the practice of education presents the interested observer with a curious mixture of essential and nonessential elements. It offers a hodgepodge of immanent and contingent or essential and nonessential truths. The only way of separating those two categories is by trying to say what makes something essential rather than merely contingent. And the only way of doing that is by making a case for including or excluding this or that element. Making that case is what both Dewey and Tillich are urging their readers to do, albeit in two quite separate, though not unrelated, spheres of discourse: education and theology.

Discerning what is essential in either sphere entails moving in the direction of the unconditional, or the unmoved mover, as Aristotle might say. It calls for incrementally pushing beyond the known until one is forced to concede having reached a limit. One then says things like, "This is as far as I dare go," or "This is absolutely the most important consideration to take into account," or even at times, "This I can't prove, but I nonetheless firmly believe it." For individuals in search of the essential, that final stopping point, with all the points that lead up to it, constitutes what Tillich calls "an object of ultimate concern."

Objects of ultimate concern are cultural creations that might also be called spiritual, in no way implying supernaturalism but simply meaning they cannot be determined empirically. Their totality lies beyond experience and therefore is never fully realized. Yet we can yearn for it as one yearns for perfection or as the religious believer yearns for unification with the Godhead. It can also be depicted symbolically.

In his closing remarks in *Experience and Education*, Dewey does not advocate searching for the educationally essential to anywhere near the extreme Tillich describes. He does not point out, for example, the impossibility of completing such a task. In fact, he says nothing about the difficulty. Does that mean that he doesn't think the task is difficult or that he disagrees with Tillich in some other way?

I think not, yet I'm not sure. What gives me pause is Dewey's orientation as a pragmatist, which seemingly keeps him immersed in the here and now. He often appears to be chiefly interested in getting things done, above all removing the barriers that impede action. That's a very valuable stance in many situations—eminently practical, yet closely tied to the immediate conditions. That immediacy is fundamentally empirical in its orientation. Those who work exclusively under its spell do not press relentlessly for ultimate answers.

Yet to be fair, when I read Dewey carefully I sense that he does see beyond the immediate and does care about the ultimate even when discussing educational matters, or perhaps especially then. That care is obliquely apparent in the questions he presented to his 1938 audience. It is evident elsewhere in those same lectures as well.

Consider, for example, the uncharacteristic (for Dewey) outburst that appears in the third chapter of *Experience and Education*. He is discussing the importance of "collateral learning," the name he gives to the "formation of enduring attitudes, of likes and dislikes" that he claims "may be and often is more important than the spelling lesson or lesson in geography or history that is learned." To drive that point home he pulls out all the stops and sounds a lament eloquent in its intensity yet confined to a single sentence:

> What avail is it to win prescribed amounts of information about geography and history, to win ability to read and write, if in the process the individual loses his own soul: loses his appreciation of things worth while, of the values to which these things are relative; if he loses desire to apply what he has learned and, above all, loses the ability to extract meaning from his future experiences as they occur?[1]

The four losses Dewey refers to, capped with "above all," leave little doubt that he cares very much about the damage done when an education malfunctions. Tillich, I believe, would heartily concur, for much the same reasons Dewey gives.

Another much-quoted passage in which Dewey's concern with ultimacy becomes evident is found in the closing lines of his small book *A Common Faith*, which contains his sole freestanding treatise on religion. There he writes,

---

1. John Dewey, *Experience and Education* (New York: Collier Books, 1938), XXX.

The things in civilization we most prize are not of ourselves. They exist by grace of the doings and sufferings of the continuous human community in which we are a link. Ours is the responsibility of conserving, transmitting, rectifying and expanding the heritage of values we have received that those who come after us may receive it more solid and secure, more widely accessible and more generously shared than we have received it.[2]

Although Dewey doesn't directly say so in that paragraph, his using the term "things in civilization" rather than "things in nature" makes it clear that "heritage of values" refers to cultural achievements. They are the outgrowth of creative effort by the human community. Though they may be realized materially (as they indeed must be if they are to be conserved and transmitted), they are basically ideational or, if you will, spiritual in origin. That ideational or spiritual starting place implies infinitude. It means their totality remains open in a dual sense—to both rectification and expansion.

Rectification deals with error. Its motion is circular; it backtracks and undoes a portion of what has been done so as to move closer to the truth. It executes the maneuver summarized in the German term *Aufhebung*, which I have discussed. Expansion has to do with growth. It moves horizontally, adding incrementally to what has already been accomplished and understood.

Conserving, transmitting, rectifying, and expanding typify what goes on between a teacher and her students when instruction is under way. Those same four moves typify what goes on at the forefront of scholarship and research, where fresh discoveries and crucial revisions are constantly being made. There is an important difference, however, between the interpersonal exchanges in the average classroom, especially at the lower levels of education, and the far more pioneering work of adding to human knowledge in toto and advancing its cutting edge. The difference is that what is being rectified and expanded in the classroom is usually limited to the students' idiosyncratic grasp of what is being taught. The scholar or the scientific

2. John Dewey, *A Common Faith* (New Haven, CT: Yale University Press, 1934), 87.

investigator rectifies and expands knowledge as it exists for everyone, at least potentially. That total expanse of knowledge constitutes what most people refer to as its "body." Mastering this body of knowledge in any particular field of human endeavor qualifies a person as an expert.

The difference between the routine rectifying and expanding in classrooms and what takes place in advanced laboratories and scholarly institutions can easily lead to difficulty when high-level experts in the various fields are called on to advise teachers. It has indeed done so, most notably in the curriculum reform movement of the 1960s and 1970s when experts from research universities and elsewhere were given the task of refashioning the curriculum of elementary and secondary schools. The results, in the main, were disappointing if not disastrous.

The experts were chiefly concerned with the abstract structure of knowledge (what we have been calling its essence), whereas teachers' concerns are more divided and somewhat more mundane. Teachers are certainly concerned with the structure of knowledge, as are the experts, for in the end that is what they aim to conserve and transmit. But they are also concerned with how that knowledge rests with those they teach. To that end, they are often called on to be judgmental about what their students say and do. That is where the pedagogical manifestation of rectifying and expanding finds its place.

In coming to terms with the embryonic and imperfect state of their students' knowledge, teachers almost invariably face a mixture of right and wrong. I call that condition *existential* simply because it exists, not because it has any profound philosophical meaning. It is based on experience and can be empirically verified by testimony, but its imperfection calls for modification. Essence and existence await separation. Yet, oddly enough, they also beg to be unified, if not at once, at least in the long run. Immediate pedagogical intervention is required, even though its ultimate goal in some idealized sense may turn out to be unreachable.

The task of separating essence and existence sounds straightforward enough, especially when reduced to the mundane business of commenting on something a student has said or done—approving it, correcting it, and so forth. That comes close to describing what most teachers do day in and day out. Yet this chapter began by describing the essence/existence task in rather lofty terms, comparing it to the way a leading theologian like Paul Tillich systematically addresses the aims of theology. To complicate matters, I suggested that both Tillich and Dewey were tacitly endorsing an impossible quest: a search for final answers to questions that have no final answers. That noble, if ultimately futile, pursuit, I implied, also describes what teachers are up to much of the time, whether they realize it or not.

LOFTY AND MUNDANE VIEWS OF TEACHING

We thus have two images of a teacher's calling that appear to be at odds: one exalted, the other mundane; one fanciful, the other more matter-of-fact. Is there a way of reconciling those images, of bringing them together? Or might they represent alternative perspectives that serve quite different purposes and thus are best kept apart?

I want to answer yes to both questions. I believe the two images *can* be unified and actually become so from time to time for individual teachers as well as their students. That happy outcome may even occur often. But I also insist on the distinction between the mundane and the exalted as outlooks on teaching and on life in general. Thus there are good reasons for keeping them separate, at least conceptually.

Let's start with the exalted image, which portrays teachers and students as nobly engaged in an impossible task. Once again, what is that task? Why is it impossible? And what makes it noble?

The task, I have said, is basically one of getting to the truth of things, of untangling essence and existence. In that formulation "essence" stands for unadulterated truth and "existence" stands for a mixture of truth and untruth. Essence is what we're looking for. Existence is what we have to work with. What makes the task difficult is that truth and untruth as existing are not always easy to tell apart. Their separation often calls for close attention and argument.

What makes the task impossible is the dream of bringing it to a close, of finally arriving at "the truth, the whole truth, and nothing but the truth," as the courtroom clerk solemnly intones. The trouble is, there is no whole truth with respect to those things that matter most to us. The whole truth about them doesn't exist save as a cognitive fantasy, a mere possibility. It therefore can only be sought, not discovered.

What makes that task noble is where it leads. It points upward, toward the pinnacle of human striving and even beyond. By prompting us to exceed our limits, it aims higher than we can go. The effort it initiates and sustains leads to our making the best use of whatever powers of thought and feeling it calls into action.

Now let's look at the mundane image, which portrays teachers, at least teachers of young children, as engaged in the fairly pedestrian and undemanding task of fielding easy questions, correcting students when they give wrong answers or otherwise miss the mark, keeping an eye out for inattention, misbehavior, and so forth. Almost anyone, it seems, could manage to do those things without much difficulty and also without much thought. Even if we turn to higher levels of education the picture doesn't change dramatically. There too it's easy enough to imagine teachers performing routine tasks almost mechanically, not only day after day but year after year. To dignify such performances by calling them noble or, further, to imagine that the teachers would so characterize their labor, seems questionable indeed. And to imagine that those same teachers think of themselves as engaged in an impossible task seems equally inappropriate.

How then are we to reconcile these competing images of teaching that I have characterized as "lofty" and "mundane"? Can we solve the problem by declaring one of them true and the other false? I think not. Instead we need to see how each has its place in a balanced conception of teaching. How can we do that?

We might begin by recognizing that the lofty view of teaching need seldom be actively pondered while a teacher goes about her workaday responsibilities. Deciding the next step amid the hustle and bustle of classroom life is usually quite enough to think about.

It's even possible that such a lofty view of teaching need *never* be pondered, not only not while the fat's in the fire, so to speak, but even during moments of solitary reflection. I must demur, however, by saying that I would view such a totally noncontemplative teacher as seriously impoverished emotionally and intellectually.

But personal judgment aside, not only run-of-the-mill teachers but some of the most talented can get by for quite some time without having lofty thoughts about their work. Many surely do so regularly. I insist, however, that such a view is there to be had by all who seek to entertain it. Those who choose do so, I again opine, stand to be greatly enriched in the long run, as do their students.

Later we will see that the fullest exercise of human freedom calls on all teachers to think lofty thoughts about the overall purpose of their calling. The same holds, of course, for anyone who is trying to accomplish anything whatever that is truly worthwhile. Lofty thoughts alone hold the key to both genuine progress and true contentment. Such has been the message of sages and seers through the centuries. As Spinoza puts it at the conclusion of his *Ethics*, "All things excellent are as difficult as they are rare."[3] That age-old conviction, I now believe, is probably what drove Dewey to offer the advice that brought to a close his series of lectures in 1938. I further have come to believe that his suggestion remains as worthwhile today as it was back then.

Yet many today may be just as puzzled by that sage advice as I was when I came upon it years ago. Perhaps they currently believe, as I did then, that professional educators surely know from the start what the essence of education is, pure and simple. If that's true, there's nothing of substance to think about. But we've seen how mistaken I was back then.

But teachers who come upon that same advice today may have other reasons for being puzzled. They may fail to see what is to be gained by thinking about such highfalutin matters. What's wrong with sticking to what's practical and down-to-earth and leaving the

---

3. Benedict de Spinoza, *Ethics*, trans. George Eliot, ed. Thomas Deegan (Salzburg: Institut für Anglistik und Amerikanistik, Universität Salzburg, 1981), 278.

rest to speakers at teachers' conventions and others of their ilk? Wasn't Dewey himself a leading pragmatist of his day? And doesn't pragmatism boil down to doing what the situation calls for, to concentrating on what can be accomplished in the here and now?

That position has merit, but it's also short-sighted. It implies that one must choose between being practical and being contemplative. But that's a false choice that leads to a stultifying one-sidedness. The real problem is how to combine those two points of view in a way that forestalls such an outcome.

COMBINING THE PRACTICAL AND THE CONTEMPLATIVE

One obvious solution is mechanical: temporal isolation of those two perspectives. Thus one might choose to be practical most of the time and idealistic or contemplative on occasion. This may sound like a rather artificial arrangement, and in many ways it is, but it describes how we live much of the time. We mostly behave pragmatically, doing whatever the immediate situation demands, but we often set aside special times and places for a different behavior. During such times we consciously try to become more solemn in mood and more contemplative in spirit. We treat such isolated moments, and likewise their substance, as sacred or semisacred, embellishing them with ritual and ceremony designed to remind participants of the nobler ends they should be striving toward.

Not long ago it was the custom in most public schools in America to begin each day with "opening exercises." In the school I attended, that morning ritual included a flag salute and the Pledge of Allegiance, a patriotic song, a brief reading from the Bible, and the recitation of the Lord's Prayer. For a host of reasons that hardly require rehashing here, that custom has largely disappeared from today's schools. Very few of today's more enlightened educators, I suspect, would welcome it back. I concur with that judgment.

Yet it is fairly easy to see what that largely abandoned ritual was meant to do. It was designed to grace each day's activity with an aura of solemnity right from the start. It pointed to a set of higher purposes that compulsory school attendance supposedly served. Those purposes, involving patriotic loyalty and religious sentiments, were not spelled out in detail. They were acknowledged more symbolically and aesthetically than explicitly, by gesture, words, and song. Yet their affective meaning, at least in gross terms, came across unequivocally, even to those of us who were so young we could barely understand what was being said or sung.

The mechanical solution to resolving the relation between the practical and contemplative approaches to education clearly has its merits. Moreover, although "opening exercises" may have largely disappeared in grade schools, the strategy of setting aside a special time and place for the contemplative is still widely practiced at all levels of education. Consider, as the classic case, the ubiquity of graduation ceremonies.

What are such ceremonies for? They obviously provide an occasion to celebrate graduates' accomplishments in the admiring presence of family and friends. The academic dress, the music and speeches, the pomp and circumstance add to the solemnity. Consider also the physical paraphernalia that goes with such ceremonies: the diplomas, certificates, ribbons, rings, pins, yearbooks, photographs, and all the rest of it. What function do those objects serve? They are tangible reminders of the intangible, visible tokens that stand for the transcendent, the unconditional, for what cannot be seen, heard, or touched. In sum, the graduation ceremony with all its hoopla is specifically designed to bring months or even years of educational striving to a fitting close.

Yet there remains something arbitrary and artificial about all such mechanical solutions to the problem of combining the practical and the contemplative. The class rings and letter sweaters may be worn with pride for years and the diplomas displayed on office walls or hung in the sanctuary of one's study for close to a lifetime, but those objects too seldom occasion what is highly desirable yet artificially sought: a mode of contemplation that genuinely adheres to what was accomplished and to much else as well. To overcome that artificiality we need a more dynamic solution, one that moves beyond the harsh temporal boundaries demonstrated in the spring graduation ceremony. Moving beyond those boundaries brings the two perspectives much closer together, even to the point of overlap. For teachers and students alike, that proximity has its usual setting in the immediacy of classroom life.

What would such a dynamic solution look like? How would it be evinced in action? Its chief characteristic, I'd say, would be a habit of transparency, of seeing beyond the immediacy of whatever happens to be the current focus of thought and action. Within cognitive psychology this tendency to leapfrog, to transcend limits intellectually, was sometimes called "divergent" thinking to differentiate it from "convergent" thinking, which was supposedly much more focused and goal-oriented. Those terms have gone out of fashion, but the general idea remains valid.

In a classroom characterized by a dynamic solution to the practical/contemplative dichotomy there would be frequent divergence from the straight and narrow. The unexpected would occur more often. Thoughts would tend to wander, both publicly and privately. Yet such digressions would not be signs of escape from boredom. They would indicate that thought was being taken seriously, afforded the freedom to seek its own limit. I'll have more to say on this notion of freedom in due course.

We now have three pairs of terms whose polarities we've been juggling for quite some time: *essence/existence*, *lofty/mundane*, and *practical/contemplative*. With their help we principally have concluded that the pursuit of truth entails the separation of essence and existence; that the work of teaching may be viewed from either a lofty or a mundane perspective; and that education as a whole may be looked at from either a practical or a contemplative point of view. Those three conclusions by themselves are not very exciting, but they become vastly more so when we add the warning, inspired largely by Hegel, that all three pairs of terms invite disaster when either of the members is treated in isolation. The task at all times, we thus have concluded, is basically dialectical. It requires coming to terms with the relation of the two sides of each pair rather than trying to choose between them. An either/or solution just doesn't work.

Now it's time to add yet another pair of terms to the mix, one I think has special significance for teachers. The pair to be added

derives chiefly from the writings of Paul Tillich, although they
are frequently mentioned by Dewey, who names them somewhat
differently.

SHAPING AND RECEIVING AS PEDAGOGICAL
STRATEGIES

Early in his discussion of the structure of reason in *Systematic Theology*, Tillich talks about "grasping and shaping the world." He writes,
"The mind receives and reacts. In receiving reasonably, the mind
grasps its world; in reacting reasonably, the mind shapes its world."
"Grasping," in this context, has the connotation of penetrating the
depth, the essential nature of a thing or an event, of understanding
and expressing it. "Shaping" has the connotation of transforming a
given material into a gestalt, a living structure that has the power of
being.

He continues, "The division between the grasping and the shaping character of reason is not exclusive. In every act of reasonable reception an act of shaping is involved, and in every act of reasonable
reaction an act of grasping is involved. We transform reality according to the way we see it, and we see reality according to the way we
transform it. Grasping and shaping the world are interdependent."[4]

For Tillich, those two activities of grasping and shaping (he often substitutes "receiving" for "grasping") not only characterize the
structure of reason but also stand for two fundamentally different
cognitive strategies. One strategy, "grasping" or "receiving," is basically appreciative. It calls, Tillich says, for "the creative union of two
natures, that of knowing and that of the known."[5] The other strategy, "shaping" or "reacting," is basically assertive. It calls for taking
control of both what is known and the process of knowing. The affective tenor of the two activities also differs. The grasping strategy

---

4. Paul Tillich, *Systematic Theology*, vol. 1 (Chicago: University of Chicago Press,
1951), 76.
    5. Ibid., 103.

tends to be more sympathetic and emotional; the shaping strategy is more aloof and impersonal.

Dewey's Version of the Two Activities

In his many accounts of how thinking proceeds as a human endeavor, Dewey frequently employs a set of terms akin to those of shaping and receiving. He calls them "doing" and "undergoing." They characterize the two-step process that governs scientific inquiry and, by implication, almost all thinking. Here is how Dewey commonly employs those terms. Faced with an empirical problem, he explains, the person in such a fix first surveys the situation, taking into account all the relevant facts. That constitutes the initial "undergoing" phase. The problem solver then decides on a remedy and promptly puts that design into action. That's the "doing" phase. If the plan works, well and good. Case closed. If not, the problem solver steps back and reexamines the situation to see what needs to be done next. That's a recurrence of the "undergoing" phase followed, needless to say, by some more "doing." And so it goes, Dewey tells us. The problem solver seesaws interminably between "doing" and "undergoing" until the problem is finally solved or deemed unsolvable.

There is of course much to be said in favor of such a picture of how thinking works. We humans do indeed seesaw between doing and undergoing when faced with many, if not most of life's problems. That back-and-forth motion marks us as rational beings. Indeed, it is the hallmark of our rationality.

The trouble is that Dewey's two-step model is far too simplistic. It works pretty well in describing how we behave when faced with an empirical problem that yields to a quick solution, such as fixing a flat tire or deciding what route to take to our destination. It works much less well as the problem grows more complex. This growth happens rapidly when the situation takes on shades of social, political, or interpersonal coloration. As complexities of that nature enter the scene, the twin modes of response that Dewey identifies as "doing and undergoing" suddenly sound too one-dimensional, too wooden and mechanical, to accommodate the nuances of the situation. It is only in the light of those new social and interpersonal demands that we begin to see the true difference between "receiving" and "controlling"—or preferably "receiving" and "*shaping*," whose softer tone comes closer to expressing what teachers are engaged in.

"Receiving," as it takes place in teaching, largely consists of listening attentively to whatever one's students say and do, while looking on appreciatively and trying to understand sympathetically what *they* understand as they struggle to come to their own grasp of the matter. That kind of listening and looking, when successful, gives the teacher a knowledge that is intimate and personal. Tillich calls it "receiving knowledge." It embodies a truth that is fundamentally *empathic*, which the dictionary defines as "allowing one to identify oneself mentally with a person or thing and so understand his feelings or its meaning." In short, it is a way of participating in another person's life.

"Shaping," as it occurs in teaching, takes two principal forms, though it is not always easy to tell them apart. One is far more overt than the other. Teachers undertake the former quite consciously most of the time; the latter, much less so.

The more overt shaping largely consists of correcting students' errors and of passing along new information in words and visual displays of various kinds. Those two modes of influence echo the "rectifying and expanding" that Dewey spoke of at the close of *A Common Faith*. Their combination forms the warp and woof of direct instruction.

The less overt shaping manifests itself in a variety of ways. The most common is modeling. Most simply, teachers serve as models to be admired and emulated. In their actions and demeanor they exemplify virtue. To their students their knowledge may seem boundless. Their patience, their sense of fairness, their attitude of calm reflection, even their displays of humor in some cases, stand out as attributes worth copying. Such qualities have shaping force, as many former students will readily testify.

Of course, negative instances of teachers' influence likewise abound. Not every teacher is a paragon, as we all know. Some are cruel and mean-spirited. Others exemplify sloth and bad manners.

Those undesirable attributes have their effect on students, at times even more enduringly than their desirable traits. But these effects are not properly classified as "shaping," even when they are lasting. For the marks they leave in students' memories are more like deformations than formations. They serve as reminders of what teachers should *not* be rather than as models of what the students might someday become.

Doing unto Others in a Shaping Mode

All such positive shaping, whether overtly or covertly accomplished, is indeed a form of "doing," as Dewey says. But it is far more than that. It is a very special kind of doing, whose ultimate recipient is a fellow human and that seeks to change its recipient in a way that will be of lasting benefit to the individual and to society at large. The knowledge it takes to do that shaping is partially impersonal and technical, and to that extent it can be codified, verified, and practiced in a fairly mechanical fashion. Tillich calls that portion "controlling knowledge." But the control it employs needs to be tempered by knowledge that can only be gained experientially, by participating with others directly and intimately. Tillich calls that portion "receiving knowledge." Having given them separate names, he stresses the necessity of combining those two forms of knowledge when dealing with others. "Physicians, psychotherapists, educators, social reformers and political leaders," he says, "deal with that side of a life-process which is individual, spontaneous, and total. They can work only on the basis of a knowledge which unites controlling and receiving elements. The truth of their knowledge is verified partly by experimental test, partly by a participation in the individual life with which they deal."[6]

The need to combine "controlling" and "receiving" knowledge gives teachers, along with workers in the other helping professions Tillich names, the recurrent task of alternating between being assertive and being accepting. The affective tone that accompanies those alternations also tends to differ. Controlling knowledge calls for

6. Ibid.

being relatively cool and impersonal, maybe even somewhat aloof. Receiving knowledge calls for being closer to warm and friendly. Those differences are not absolute, of course, but they do require teachers to switch gears emotionally as they move from a controlling to a receiving mode, or the reverse. Moreover, this often must happen in the blink of an eye.

But it is not enough to say that educators join physicians, psychotherapists, and others in having to combine controlling and receiving knowledge. They must do more. They must combine those two forms of knowledge in the interest of preserving and sharing an even higher form of knowledge, which transcends the controlling and receiving and gives them purpose. In *A Common Faith* Dewey refers to that higher form of knowledge as "the things in civilization we most prize."[7]

That "heritage of values," as Dewey also calls it, extends beyond the individual transactions between teachers and students. It is what gives those transactions content. Educators call that content "subject matter." Another word for its entirety might be the "goods" of the world, with the meaning of "goods" raised to the highest level of universality. Actually, Dewey's alternative term, "the heritage of values," is not quite accurate. The heritage is not of "values" alone; it is *an understanding of what is valued and treated with respect* by a particular social community. It is what is accepted as normative and even close to obligatory as knowledge by that community. It further entails an invitation to participate in that community by accepting those norms.

7. Dewey, *Common Faith*, 87.

5   Making Subjects Matter

Educators' customary use of the term "subject matter" sometimes leads to confusion, and it therefore requires clarification. Despite its use as a compound noun, "subject matter" is not a singular entity. Nor is it an identifiable attribute of any body of knowledge treated in isolation. Rather, the meaning of its two parts is always relational. It refers to what "matters" to someone. For that person a particular "subject" (internally represented) or "object" (externally observed) becomes a focus that she momentarily chooses to investigate further. Seen in this light, the goal of education in the short term becomes selecting a "subject" or "object" that will ultimately come to "matter" (be of interest) to both the teacher and her students.

Usually this means starting with something that already interests the teacher and making it interesting to students. Often that task is readily accomplished, for the mere fact that it interests her usually makes it of some interest to those present. But as every teacher knows, that is by no means always true. Making a subject that "matters" to oneself "matter" to someone else sometimes takes a lot of doing.

To say that something "matters" to people is to say they find it of concern. Put somewhat differently, it is also to say that it interests them. But as we know, concern, interest, and "mattering," along with other such terms that might apply, can vary greatly in intensity. A person can be mildly concerned or greatly concerned, slightly interested or intensely interested. Something can matter a lot or hardly matter at all.

As those feelings intensify, they move toward a degree of ultimacy that easily defies ordinary description. We then speak of the object of concern in terms reserved for the things we love. We say things like "I don't just care who wins that game, I care passionately" or, to put such a feeling in an educational context, "I'm not just interested in history, I *love* history!"

Such a declaration of love affixed to an ordinary school subject raises the obvious question, Should education aspire to having all students love everything they're taught? "Of course not," we teachers all must aver. Such a goal is clearly unattainable. But educators should aspire to having every school subject *matter* at least minimally to the students they serve. Moreover, whatever is being studied should come to matter, at least in part, for its *intrinsic* worth and not simply because mastery is required by the powers that be or because it is believed to be instrumental to attaining some other goal, such as earning high grades or winning the teacher's approval or even opening the doors to higher aspirations.

Beyond aspiring to have every school subject *matter* at least minimally to students, there are two further turns on "mattering" that all educators would do well to consider. The first is that education as a whole publicly heralds the unbounded nature of what Dewey calls "the things in civilization we most prize." It toots its own horn on behalf of the infinite wonders of the world. It does so through the sheer variety of its offerings, their plenitude standing as mute testimony to the encyclopedic scope of all that is worthy of study. This is why the curriculum of the lower schools offers its students a rich introductory sampling of the world's prized possessions. That diversity is designed to be more than eye-opening. It is meant to be mind-boggling—to occasion a kind of spiritual awakening. Its goal, in short, is to make more things matter.

The second thing to consider with respect to "mattering" in general is that in a variety of ways education makes clear how very far one may possibly go in pursuit of something that matters. Many key courses, for example, require prolonged study. From the earliest grades forward subjects like math and English are revisited year after year. Advancement in them, students soon learn, takes a lot of time. Even those who do the instructing are still learners. Teachers usually know considerably more about what is being taught than their students do, but they seldom are perched near the forward edge of that knowledge. Beyond them sit authors of textbooks and the creators of other teaching materials. Far closer to the edge are scholars and researchers of international renown. But even they do not have the final word on any matter of serious consequence. There always remains more to be learned and perhaps some things to be unlearned ("rectified," as Dewey might say).

But it is not just the open-ended nature of learning that education's treatment of what "matters" prompts us to consider. Education's presentation of subject matter opens doors that point the way to future pursuits and invite further exploration. Therein lies their promise.

For when pursued diligently and sufficiently, what matters most to a person for an extended time often becomes a way of life. It defines that person's identity. Individuals who follow such a arduous pursuit wind up standing tall within a world of their own making. What matters most to them becomes their vocation. Their occupation bears its name. Its full expression encompasses the entire range of their deepest and most enduring interests.

To the extent that other conditions allow their expression, all such life-enhancing choices bear witness to the human capacity to act freely, to create rather than be acted upon by either the external forces of nature or the internal forces of impulse and desire. That capacity to exercise freedom rationally, along with the propensity to do so, is another of the conditions education seeks to foster. I now turn to a poetic expression of what it means to exercise that freedom.

STEVENS'S "PASTORAL NUN"

The collected work of Wallace Stevens contains a short poem that relates in important ways to the topic of this chapter and, even more important, to the theme of this book as a whole. Here is "A Pastoral Nun" in its entirety.

> Finally, in the last year of her age,
> Having attained a present blessedness,
> She said poetry and apotheosis are one.
>
> This is the illustration that she used:
> If I live according to this law I live
> In an immense activity, in which
>
> Everything becomes morning, summer, the hero,
> The enraptured woman, the sequestered night,
> The man that suffered, lying there at ease,
>
> Without his envious pain in body, in mind,
> The favorable transformation of the wind
> As of a general being or human universe.
>
> There was another illustration, in which
> The two things compared their tight resemblances:
> Each matters only in that which it conceives.

Most striking as the poem relates to this chapter is its last line, which contains the chapter's key word: *matters*. "Each matters only in that which it conceives," the nun finally declares. Read at one level, then, the poem as a whole is about making things matter, which is also what this chapter is about. The trick, we learn from the nun, is to exalt the importance of everything. She accomplishes that crucial objective by elevating in her mind's eye all she witnesses—the time of day, the season of the year, the people she meets, the hush of night, her own religious imagery—even the wind comes to life when favorably transformed by her fertile imagination. She really works at it. She *conceives* what matters. It germinates within her like a developing embryo. She gives birth to Beauty daily by actively seeking what each thing stands for when viewed in the best possible light. That activity, obviously a labor of love, yields more than artifice. It changes the producer as much as the product, the subject as much as the object. It issues from a mature understanding of art's mission. It also, as the good sister makes clear, reflects a deep understanding of religion. That dual insight accounts for her opening proclamation, that poetry and apotheosis are one.

There is, of course, something a bit much, even over the top, about the nun's projected endorsement of the "law" she has finally come upon. Her planned compliance with that law is far too extreme. She can't really mean what she says. *Everything* can't become morning, summer, the hero, and all the rest of it, no matter how hard she might try to make that happen. Only some things can undergo such a change. Moreover, most of the time those cherished transformations take place only momentarily. With a shake of the head, a harsher view of reality generally returns, even for those of us who are most strongly inclined to follow the nun's lead. Life's drabness, its humdrum aspects, rarely disappears completely, save for those famous fictional characters, such as Voltaire's Candide or Cervantes's Don Quixote, whose starry-eyed vision turns out to be deeply tragic in the long run.

Yet the nun's opening announcement and her plan to act on it remain important all the same, especially for educators. Her projected activity, even if grossly exaggerated, stands as an apt reminder of something that many, if not most, good teachers do almost automatically. They routinely look on the bright side of their students' scholarly efforts. Moreover, they do so from the very start. That is how they begin their response to whatever their students offer in the way of oral commentary and written work. They treat it at first as a cup half full rather than half empty. They applaud what is often paltry in quality, making it appear better than it actually is.

Does that almost instinctive way of behaving entail a touch of dishonesty on the teacher's part? Yes and no. It does call for being predominantly upbeat and generous in one's approach to students. That dominant attitude is not always easy to maintain, I grant. It may require a fib or two. To put it in terms that have become clichéd, rose-colored glasses are often called for when teachers react to their students' work. That handy optical device should remain ready for use daily, if not hourly.

But teachers' responsibility requires that they take off those rose-colored glasses when it comes time to render constructive criticism, often on the heels of a compliment. Indeed, the "glasses on/glasses off" routine is such a normal part of teaching that most teachers can perform it in a twinkling. In judging the honesty of such a performance, the important thing is that the teacher's change from a smile to a straight face or even a frown is not just stagecraft, or at least it needn't be. Both can be genuine expressions of how the teacher feels about the student's effort. Praise and criticism can be honestly mixed. Many teachers become quite artful in concocting and serving that mixture. The positive aspect of their art, the "glasses on" part, thus becomes the educational equivalent of the nun's plan for action. That's the most obvious message that the seasoned teacher, looking for support of her routine way of behaving, might readily draw from the Stevens poem.

But does the poem contain an even larger message for educators? I think it might, which leads me to say that its content, when reflected upon, relates to the theme of this book in important ways both small and large.

Consider, as a small start, the poem's opening word: *Finally*. I love the abruptness of that beginning. Coming as a bit of a surprise, it alerts the reader that the story is in midstream. Something has been going on for some time. The reader immediately wants to know what has been going on before the tale's impending close.

That's the way Stevens starts several of his poems. He puts first things last and last things first. He is fond of drawing poetic circles. That circular motion harks back to our discussion of the way thought moves. It too spins like a top. It keeps returning to its starting place. As another poet, Jane Hirshfield, has even more recently proclaimed: "Any point of a circle is its start: desire forgoing fulfillment to go on desiring."[1] Desire desiring to continue, just as thought does.

Notice also in the poem's first line that the nun was in the last year of her *age* when she attained her present blessedness. She was not in the last year of her *life*. We are not being told the story of a nun who had long ago passed on. At least at the time the poet spoke

---

1. Jane Hirshfield, "Sentencings," *Poetry*, December 2010, 211.

to her this nun was very much alive. We hear her words. Her present blessedness, the poem implies, had rejuvenated her. She was not only still living but had miraculously stopped *aging*. Those accustomed to religious language might say she had been reborn. That too is something that thought, at least thought of a certain kind, is said to be able to accomplish. It sometimes offers a new lease on life.

What kinds of thought might conduce to the present blessedness of rejuvenation? Traditionally, as in Stevens's poem, the answer comes couched in religious terms. The familiar phrase "born-again Christian" pops instantly to mind when the talk turns to such experiences. But are those the only kind of thoughts that might have such power? I venture that they may not be.

To those religious thoughts reputed to be rejuvenating I would add a much larger and more inclusive class of thinking, one containing thoughts that themselves remain young, at least figuratively. But what kind of thoughts might those be? The quick answer is that they must be *young* thoughts—thoughts that lie on the outermost fringe of thinking, thoughts that are new to the thinker herself.

But to address more fully the kind of thoughts that keep us young, we need to shift gears. I suggested earlier that the content of Stevens's poem relates to the theme of this book in both small and large ways. We have just considered a few of the smaller ways; now we need turn to some of the larger ones.

EXTENDING THE PURVIEW OF THE NUN'S TALE

Stevens calls his nun "pastoral," meaning, I suppose, that she behaves rather like a pastor. She preaches to her listeners. Within the narrow confines of her few spoken lines she offers a tiny sermon, containing a piece of sage advice whose bottom line, though unstated, is clearly addressed to her listeners. It says, in effect: "Go hence and do likewise." In light of that firm advice, which sounds rather homiletic, shall we call Stevens's nun a *preacher* or a *teacher*? She seems to me a bit of both. Perhaps all teachers share that fundamental duality.

The seminal insight her advice springs from is straightforward. It simply declares that art and religion closely resemble each other.

But what follows from that rudimentary generalization is what truly matters. For this particular nun, the close relation between art and religion entails a moral obligation. It obliges her to look at the world differently than she had been doing, to see it afresh in both religious and artistic terms. That kind of seeing calls for a moral renewal in the poem's readers as well. It urges all who would heed her example to see things not just freshly but positively or, adding a touch of romantic sentiment to that Norman Vincent Peale type of advice, to see them lovingly.

But there is more to that somewhat saccharine advice than rank sentiment. The nun is not just urging her listeners to adopt a lovey-dovey attitude toward the world in general. She is saying something far more important than that. She is at least hinting at what adopting such an attitude must entail if one is to eschew mawkish sentimentality. Its realization demands an active search for something that is not yet fully attained and perhaps only dimly perceived, if visible at all. That "something," expressed in a single word, might best be called perfection. Seek perfection in all things, the nun tacitly urges, and you will begin to sense its presence even in the most unlikely places and with respect to some of the least likely objects.

The nun's primary message focuses exclusively on the close relation between art and religion, but its focus could easily be broadened to include a vast number of other human activities. Philosophy and morals come first to mind, of course, because of their close affinity with the historical evolution of both art and religion. Those four broad domains—art, religion, philosophy, and morals—are followed quickly in historical sequence by scholarly studies in general, including, of course, all the sciences. Though vast and varied as an assortment of human endeavors, all such wide-ranging activities share a family resemblance. Each points toward the unattainable. The dedicated practitioners in each of those domains aspires to a level of perfection that lies forever out of reach.

What of education as a human endeavor? Does it deserve to be included in that distinguished company of seekers after perfection? I would certainly say it does, most emphatically so. And I expect that almost all professional educators would agree. Those outside critics who adopt a snootier view and tend to look down on education would doubtless disagree, but that's *their* problem. They're simply misinformed. They haven't given the matter sufficient thought. Education doesn't yet *matter* enough to them.

Finally, when we muse for long enough on the content of Stevens's poem and its connection to the theme of this book, we belatedly come to see, if I'm not mistaken, that the poem's last line almost perfectly expresses the unspoken conviction that must have lain behind Dewey's 1938 advice to his audience of educators. He knew in his day and sought to convince others that the only way to make education truly matter, first as a concept and then as a reality, is to examine it with care—in a word, lovingly. Only then does its underlying importance, and with that its intrinsic goodness, truth, and beauty, begin to shine forth.

6　In Pursuit of Perfection

Chapter 2, which dealt with the notion of trafficking in truth as a way of depicting education's task, began, "Leaving aside for a time education's highest truth . . ." The phrase "for a time" implicitly promised a return to what had been put on hold. Now I must deliver on that promise. Education's highest truth awaits immediate disclosure.

The trouble is, the task is far trickier than one might guess, for education's highest truth has no tangible existence. It is not something that can be examined empirically. It can only be thought about, talked about, gestured toward. The situation calls to mind the familiar scene in a cowboy movie where the wizened old geezer points in the direction taken by the pair of outlaws astride galloping horses that have long disappeared from sight. "They went thataway!" is about all he can tell the band of pursuers, with a sweep of his arm.

To those in pursuit of education's highest truth, the old geezer could point in only one direction: straight up. His raised forefinger would say it all. Education's ultimate goal, its highest truth, can only be perfection.

But that upward gesture, even if accurate as a signpost, is not very satisfying. Perfection may be the ultimate target, true enough. It may establish unequivocally the direction education is always headed, but how does that indisputable destination play out in real life? What does it call on educators to do? What are its curricular implications?

Answering such questions in full would require a book of its own. To address them even in a preliminary way is daunting. The path we shall now take is roundabout, even a bit mazelike, I fear. It weaves back and forth between present and past and also veers far afield from the notion of perfection per se. It is, in short, a kind of free association response to the cluster of questions that the thought of perfection as it applies to education inspires.

I will start with a brief look at the dual concepts of *freedom* and *norms* as explicated by the theologian Paul Tillich. Then I'll turn back to Dewey's closing words to his audience of educators in 1938, the enigmatic announcement that served as a springboard for my own fledgling effort. From there we'll jump even further back in time to have a look at a document Dewey wrote some forty years earlier, while he was busy founding the University of Chicago's Laboratory School. I'll bring the chapter to its close by considering the curricular implications of the preceding discussion, particularly as they touch on the importance of humanistic studies.

FREEDOM AS OPENNESS TO NORMS OF UNCONDITIONAL VALIDITY

The heading above summarizes a fuller exposition of its meaning as given by Paul Tillich in volume 3 of his *Systematic Theology*. There Tillich explains that it is through the intimate interaction of individual freedom and social norms that the moral significance of human thought and action is determined. Though his explanation serves a theological purpose, which drives all three volumes of his work, it also seems well suited to advance our thinking about the importance of both freedom and norms in educational affairs, a topic of consequence to every teacher and school official.

Tillich's starting place, shared by many if not most of today's political and social philosophers, declares that genuine freedom is not simply the absence of constraint. It is not, in other words, the libertarian's unfettered freedom of individuals to do as they please. Rather, it is freedom to follow the dictates of reason itself, bolstered and informed by the opinion of others as manifested in the dominant ethos of one's local community as well as the broader society. It is that community and that society with its many partitions and subdivisions that basically establish the norms to be followed.

Those norms all point in one direction. They point toward the truth, broadly conceived. They tell all who attend them what the well-informed citizen, or the well-informed practitioner of any guild or profession, or the person in charge of any undertaking, for that matter, believes is true with respect to this or that. Moreover, they often do more. They expand on that minimal guidance by offering explanations that purportedly tell *why* such and such is taken to be true. Those expanded norms provide an elaborate rationale for staying in step with the measured cadence of well-informed citizens and the society at large.

But those same norms, whether brief or elaborate, also do something else, something that often goes unnoticed. They point not solely toward the truth as currently conceived and practiced. Such down-to-earth truths are merely empirical; they exist under current conditions. But when viewed sub specie aeternitatis—in its essential nature—the state to which all normative conditions tacitly aspire, the targeted end point exceeds the limits of those extant conditions. It points toward the *totality* of truth with respect to this or that. That totality, as I've noted, always transcends reality. It is ideal. It does not exist, save imperfectly. Conjoined with existence, virtually interlarded with it, it constitutes that elusive quality known as essence. Hence emerges the perennial problem of having to tease out the difference between essence and existence whenever we seek the deepest of truths.

Now we are in a position to consider what Tillich's "norms of unconditional validity" might stand for in an educational context. In brief and in general, they stand for the ends sought by all human striving for perfection. They represent the end point of all those faraway goals that humans dream of and work for but seldom if ever reach. Customarily those highest of aspirations are epitomized in the philosopher's familiar triad of the Good, the True, and the Beautiful. Every schoolchild soon comes to know, at least in a rudimentary sense, the meaning of each of those key terms. Every child also soon comes to appreciate the power of those terms when issued as human judgments by those in authority. To earn such judgments from teachers and parents, to receive them as rewards for their own juvenile doings, soon becomes a universal aspiration of almost every youngster. That aspiration, when properly cultivated, becomes an enduring disposition. It then channels the use of one's freedom from that point forward. It leads to a desire to do one's best in everything, to pursue the Good, the True, and the Beautiful perpetually, and to applaud such actions by others.

The "openness" Tillich mentions highlights an aspect of human freedom that requires emphasis. It reminds us that the direction freedom takes is always optional, at least in part. Its exercise ultimately depends on the individual. Acting freely, a person may or may not persistently pursue norms of unconditional validity. He may pursue such positive goals but only half-heartedly and on occasion, or possibly not at all. Some individuals may even move in the opposite direction, performing acts that are downright destructive and evil, seriously damaging themselves and others. That too is a possible outcome of being free. Thus, as Tillich's phrase indicates, the condition of freedom only leaves humans "open" to moving toward the realization of those values that are most prized by humankind in general. Whether individuals move in that direction or finally turn against it depends in no small measure on what happens to them in the course of their education.

The option of moving toward norms of unconditional validity also has its downside. When pressed too far, it inevitably leads to disappointment, for unconditional validity turns out to be illusory. It is never fully attained. That sad fact is summed up in the aphorism "the best is the enemy of the good." The best implies perfection. When brooded on excessively, the very thought of it breeds discontent. Avoiding that outcome calls for only one solution—stopping short of disappointment. This means resting content with some version of what is, for a time, good enough, while acknowledging that despite its merits the end product could have been better. Every teacher must learn to walk that fine line daily in her instructional exchanges, and she must help her students do the same. That task calls for balanced judgment, marked by a judicious blend of appreciation and criticism from teachers and students alike.

Let's step back now for a better look at where our discussion of the pursuit of perfection has taken us. The central point has been that a striving for perfection cannot help but be a part of becoming educated. As a goal, perfection is universally sought, even when not consciously articulated. Yet the intensity of that motivation must be monitored to avoid its debilitating effect. One way of doing this is for individuals so engaged to simply try to do their best instead of aiming for perfection in some absolute sense. Athletes in training do that all the time. They strive daily for a *personal* best, whatever their sport. That same option is available to students at all levels of education. With proper encouragement from teachers and others it can become habitual.

Another way of avoiding the shoals of disappointment that threaten excessive striving is to concentrate on correcting *im*perfection. The patience required invariably pays off, for gradually eliminating those minuscule faults that serially come to one's attention offers the only true path to perfection. Traveling that path becomes arduous at times, true enough. Moreover, the best way to measure progress is by looking backward—not always easy to do. Here too the help of those who have witnessed that progress from the sidelines and might have helped to bring it about often comes in handy.

Those two strategies of constant encouragement combined with the gradual correction of emergent imperfections come about as close as one can get, it appears, to a overall summary of how today's teachers typically deal with the almost inborn striving for perfection their students evince.

DEWEY'S CLOSING STATEMENT REVISITED

Now let's return to our own starting place: Dewey's advice to his audience of educators. The unattainable though immensely attractive goal of perfection lies at the heart of that advice. Dewey was asking his listeners, later his readers, to move toward that unattainable goal by inviting them to think about the *essence* of education, what it is *essentially*.

He ends by emphasizing "the need for a sound philosophy of experience," but that emphasis on experience is clearly off the mark. For it was not *experience* he was asking his audience to think about, it was *education*. He was asking them to think of education *conceptually*, to think about what the term stands for in its fullest sense, what it *must* stand for if it is to be worthy of being called education.

That kind of thinking entails the notion of perfection, because it tries to embrace the concept totally. That means taking into consideration all its conditions, seeing it, as one might say, *un*conditionally. Only then does its totality become evident. But that unconditioned totality cannot be made manifest concretely. Why not? Because it changes over time. It is itself conditioned by historical circumstances.

The conception of education that was dominant a century or more ago is no longer dominant today. Education in Japan or France is unlike education in America in important ways. Norms change, even norms that appear to be of unconditional validity.

That's the catch-22 of Dewey's invitation. Despite our best efforts, perfection in the form of conceptual fulfillment remains forever out of reach.

Yet that shortcoming need not be a source of crippling discouragement. For despite our inability to achieve perfection in any *absolute* sense, there remain ways of inching forward. We are always free to take a *critical* look at current practices in general and at our own way of doing things. Then we are free to seek to improve those practices by taking into account matters that had escaped our attention. We thereby remain open to change. That, I'd say, is what Dewey was trying to show throughout *Experience and Education*, especially as he contrasts "progressive" and "traditional" practices.

As he points out, the "progressive" practices are not simply newer than the traditional ones, they also conform more closely to the findings of modern psychology. As Dewey depicts them, they are based on an updated conception of human cognition. That brings them closer to the truth scientifically than are the older methods. In that way they deepen our understanding of education's essence, changing it irrevocably.

Can we today come even closer to capturing education's essence than Dewey and his contemporaries did in their day? Are changes in today's norms, in what we at present think essential, still called for? That's the question Dewey invites all current readers of his text to consider. Where do we turn for an answer?

One possibility is to do as Dewey did, or as he and many of his followers thought he was doing, to turn for guidance to the empirical sciences—principally the science of psychology. Today's updated version of that option looks to neuroscience for help. "Brain research," as it is popularly called, will soon prove to be a major source of new ideas about how to teach and how to improve education generally—or so many of its supporters believe. I am not familiar enough with that research to judge its ultimate value, I must confess. I suspect, however, that it will not yield the results its strongest supporters anticipate. I offer that prediction, prejudiced though it may be, simply because I have witnessed the rise and fall of too many promises of improvement emanating from scientific and technological quarters in the recent past.

A more attractive alternative, in my opinion, calls for turning for help to what are commonly termed "the humanities." In a sense that is what Dewey was calling for as well, although to my way of thinking his talk of "a philosophy of experience" reveals the latent scientific bent of his proposal, blunting its edge. In place of looking toward psychology, I would put stronger trust in a combination of art, philosophy, and religion to deliver today's most urgently needed insight into what education is all about and how to make it better.

This humanistic approach does not exclude taking advantage of everything that both the "hard" and the "soft" empirical sciences have to offer. It continues to hold them in very high esteem, but it does subordinate their position as a primary source of insight when faced with the kind of questions Dewey put forward in his closing remarks. Those questions, as I hope my fellow explorers will by now agree, are far more conceptual than empirical. They have to do with how we should *think* about education as a highly valued human endeavor rather than with how to put such conceptions into practice. The latter set of questions are of course crucial. Without confronting them, we are only playing a game of words. But they are decidedly secondary. They come later in the game. Their answers are *grounded*, to use a term we are now familiar with, on a prior set of considerations that establish the fundamental importance of education—its *essence*, as we have come to call it—expressed unconditionally.

Why turn to art, philosophy, and religion for help in exploring those fundamental considerations? Because in those three domains our ways of thinking and acting are pushed to the edge of what we now take for granted and even a step or two beyond. The sciences exert a similar push, of course, as I've pointed out. But they do so differently. They stop short of "beyond" by remaining tied to the senses most of the way. Their expansiveness is always confined by a rigid set of empirical constraints.

Art, philosophy, and religion transcend those empirical limits, or seek to do so. They deal principally with what can never be fully experienced but can only be approximated, what I have here been referring to as the unconditional. Yet they also remain very much linked to the here and now. Each in its own way tries to bridge the gap that separates "ought to be" from "is." As Marianne Moore once said of poetry, each offers "imaginary gardens with real toads in them."

From the standpoint of thought as it typically operates in each of those three domains, the imaginary gardens usually come first and the real toads second. Or perhaps not, come to think of it. Perhaps the reverse also occurs. It may be that we are inspired to think imaginatively only by actualities. Applying that possibility to the matter at hand, perhaps it is the realized imperfections of education (including its toads, in the shape of its Mr. Gradgrinds) that lead us to think of how the enterprise as a whole (the imaginary garden) might be improved. But that conjecture exaggerates. It overworks the metaphor. The important point is that in their modus operandi art, philosophy, and religion each model the task Dewey sketched in his closing words. Moreover, as a trio they do so more vividly and more pointedly than do the empirical sciences, at least as narrowly conceived.

Oddly enough, I suspect that in his heart of hearts Dewey knew that too, even though he fails to make it clear to his audience in 1938. What leads me to that suspicion is an article Dewey wrote in 1898 as the newly appointed founder of the experimental elementary school (later named the Laboratory School) at the University of Chicago. The article, which appeared in the *School Journal*, a publication that Dewey, the school's teachers, and his university colleagues compiled and edited, bore the title "My Pedagogic Creed." In it Dewey spells out in very condensed yet elevated prose his fundamental convictions about education. His pronouncements take the form of seventy-nine brief assertions, each beginning with the phrase "I believe." It is true that that creedal statement was written long before his Kappa Delta Pi lectures: forty years earlier, to be exact. A lot can change in that time, as we know. Certainly Dewey himself changed. He went from being a young faculty member to being one of our nation's revered elder statesmen. His overall viewpoint as a philosopher, along with his outlook on education, doubtless changed as well.

Yet I can't believe he drifted so far from his earlier outlook as to divorce himself from it completely. I would wager that even in his mature years he continued to stand behind many of the key premises of his initial statement.

Perhaps the best way to communicate the tenor of those premises is to quote at some length from the both the beginning and the ending of his Pedagogic Creed and then offer some interpretation. Doing so should bring to light some of the doubts and uncertainties that dogged Dewey throughout much of his life. A number of those same tensions continue to plague our efforts today.

I should say in advance that Dewey begins by sounding like a turn-of-the-century social scientist and ends by sounding rather like a Victorian minister. That in itself I find significant. For it is chiefly in education, as Dewey makes clear, that the volatile mix of science, art, religion, and philosophy comes to a head. He also stumbles a bit at the start, as I'll point out, but soon rights himself.

DEWEY'S PEDAGOGIC CREED

"My Pedagogic Creed" opens with this paragraph:

ARTICLE ONE. WHAT EDUCATION IS
I believe that all education proceeds by the participation of the
individual in the social consciousness of the race. This process
begins unconsciously almost at birth, and is continually shaping
the individual's powers, saturating his consciousness, forming
his habits, training his ideas, and arousing his feelings and emotions. Through this unconscious education the individual gradually comes to share in the intellectual and moral resources which
humanity has succeeded in getting together. He becomes an in-
heritor of the funded capital of civilization. The most formal and
technical education in the world cannot safely depart from this
general process. It can only organize it; or differentiate it in some
particular direction.[1]

I find much to applaud in that opening statement. But I also find
it contains what seems to me a logical pratfall. What strikes me as
most laudable is Dewey's resounding declaration of the importance
of education. In its second sentence he ticks off with eloquent
brevity the potent effects of education on the individual. He then
goes on to spell out what those effects add up to in the long run.
They lead to the inheritance of what Dewey in summary calls "the
funded capital of civilization." The mercantile overtone of that tri-
umphant claim must have been especially pleasing to the ears of the
nineteenth-century titans of America's industrial strength. Its clar-
ion note of celebration still comes through loud and clear.

What troubles me is the faulty syllogism whose premises and
conclusion are deftly if somewhat surreptitiously interwoven in the
first three sentences of Dewey's statement. Let me explain.

Dewey begins with the claim that all education proceeds by the
individual's participation in the social consciousness of the race.

1. John Dewey, "My Pedagogic Creed," *School Journal* 54 (January 1897): 77–80.

Note that he does not claim that education *is* that elaborated participation. He merely notes that such is the way *education* proceeds —*as
might other forms of human interaction*, one well might add.

His second sentence begins with the words "this process." But it
is not immediately clear which process he is now referring to. Is he
speaking of "education" or is he speaking of "the participation of the
individual . . . "? As the sentence unfolds it becomes evident that he
is referring to the latter, which begins "unconsciously," as he points
out, "almost at birth." But the very next sentence makes it clear that
he has now *equated* education with that process. The two are suddenly identical. For he now speaks of "this unconscious education."

But is that move legitimate? Does it make logical sense? I think
not. In logical terms, Dewey has either unwittingly or intentionally
erased the distinction between the major and minor premises of a
categorical syllogism, making them identical in form. As a result he
has reached an erroneous conclusion. Dewey's faulty syllogism runs
like this:

1. All education proceeds by the participation of the individual in the social
   consciousness of the race.
2. Participation of the individual, etc., begins unconsciously.
3. Therefore, education begins unconsciously.

But to reach that conclusion requires as a major premise, "All participation of the individual," etc., *is* a form of education, and that
is not how Dewey begins. To reveal the flaw more dramatically, if
somewhat comically, consider the following syllogism, which echoes
Dewey's argument:

1. All cows are mortal.
2. Socrates is mortal.
3. Therefore, Socrates is a cow.

The error in that pseudologic lies in the fact that all living things
are mortal, not just cows. Humans are mortal, Socrates among them.

Analogously, much of human experience, not just education, proceeds by the participation of the individual in the social consciousness of the race. Individuals participate in that way when, for example, they post letters in the corner mailbox or order a hamburger at Wendy's or just sit and think ahead to the day's events. To label all of that participation *education*, which is the way Dewey inclines, is to dilute the meaning of the term to the point of absurdity. Preventing that dilution requires us to distinguish between those forms of participation that are worthy of the name education, as Dewey himself might say, and those that are not.

In the opening statement of his Creed Dewey hints at two criteria that promise to be of help in making that distinction. He mentions *formal* and *technical* education, which tacitly suggests that there might also be *informal* and *nontechnical* (or general) education. What do those four types of education imply? Three of them at least—formal, technical, and nontechnical—imply a conscious undertaking of some kind. Participants in each are by and large aware of being engaged in an educational enterprise. They so understand its purpose.

Informal education is somewhat more ambiguously situated as a conscious undertaking. If we think, for example, of what a child might learn just by watching his parents and other grown-ups as they go about their daily lives, we might want to call that mode of learning informal yet still educational. Perhaps that is what Dewey has in mind when he talks about the process beginning unconsciously almost at birth and when he introduces the term *unconscious education*. The notion remains fairly informal yet takes on somewhat greater consciousness, at least in the adult, when we picture a parent trying to instruct a very young child—a mother playing patty-cake with her baby, for example. Informal education then becomes more emphatically educational.

In addition to finding fault with Dewey's logical machinations, this quick gloss of the first paragraph of his Pedagogic Creed yields the key notion that education, properly conceived, is most fruitfully looked on as a conscious undertaking. Its four most prominent forms, which include informal education, are human creations through and through. They are not found in nature. Why is it important to recognize that?

It is important because it underscores that education does not just happen. It has to be planned. And those plans have to be acted on responsibly. Another way of putting this would be to say that experience alone does not educate, despite the old saw about experience being the best teacher and despite the heavy emphasis Dewey places on the linkage between experience and education.

Only certain kinds of experiences are educative, as Dewey himself was well aware. Educative experiences, on the whole, have integrity. They stand out as special in several ways. They are usually prepared for in advance, they are looked on as potentially beneficial, and they are purposefully undertaken with that benefit in mind. Their unfolding is self-consciously savored, and they subsequently are reflected on and recalled as a way of reaping their full benefit.

The trouble with the phrase *unconscious education*, which Dewey rather casually inserts in the third sentence of his Creed, is that it implies that in certain circumstances education can occur naturally, that it can take place *unconsciously*, as Dewey initially puts it. I not only disagree with that idea, I believe its effect can be pernicious if taken seriously by professional educators. It lends support to the notion that all teachers need do is surround their students with the right physical environment (an appropriately rich one, of course) and education will take care of itself. That way of thinking leads to the not uncommon practice of taking busloads of students on field trips (to an art museum, let's say) and then letting them meander about on their own without further instruction. There is nothing wrong, of course, with an unguided visit to an art museum for those who know how to treat such an occasion as an educational experience. But to imagine that all it takes is placing students in such an environment is to believe that education occurs naturally. And it most assuredly does not.

It may be that all of experience, or at least much of it, is infused with educational potential. A properly alert and well-educated person may be able to draw "lessons" from almost everything he does. But the art of self-education must be partially mastered before it can be practiced. A major goal of formal education is the cultivation of that art. Students must be taught to teach themselves, self-consciously. The early stages of that process call for the conscious guidance of others.

In sum, what occurs naturally for most humans is learning, not education. Humans learn all kinds of things, many almost effortlessly, some almost unconsciously. It is that capacity to learn that makes education possible. Much of education also requires little effort for must humans. But not all of it, not by any means. And it does not occur easily for everyone. It thus is a very conscious undertaking.

We turn now to the way Dewey concludes his Pedagogic Creed. He builds up quite a head of steam. His concluding declarations of his firm commitment to education and his belief in its importance could as appropriately be delivered from a pulpit as from a public lectern. We must keep in mind that he was writing at the close of the nineteenth century. Certain aspects of the way he expressed himself—his final hurrah, for example—are far more suited to the spirit of those days than to ours. Yet allowing for that difference, his words still resonate favorably in our own time, or so I believe.

His windup begins with a frank acknowledgment that what he has presented has been his very own idealized *conception* of education. He thus concedes its hypothetical status. He has pictured education not as it was in his day, but as it could become. He starts with, "I believe that education thus conceived marks the most perfect and intimate union of science and art conceivable in human experience." He continues with growing enthusiasm:

> I believe that the art of thus giving shape to human powers and adapting them to social service, is the supreme art; one calling into its service the best of artists; that no insight, sympathy, tact, executive power, is too great for such service.
>
> I believe that with the growth of psychological service, giving added insight into individual structure and laws of growth; and with the growth of social science, adding to our knowledge of the right organization of individuals, all scientific resources can be utilized for the purposes of education.

I believe that when science and art thus join hands the most commanding motive for human action will be reached; the most genuine springs of human conduct aroused and the best service that human nature is capable of guaranteed.

I believe, finally, that the teacher is engaged, not simply in the training of individuals, but in the formation of the proper social life.

He concludes with this:

I believe that every teacher should realize the dignity of his calling; that he is a social servant set apart for the maintenance of proper social order and the securing of the right social growth.

I believe that in this way the teacher always is the prophet of the true God and the usherer in of the true kingdom of God.

"Ba da bing!" is the kind of contemporary drumroll one wants to add to that sockaroo of a finish. A twenty-one-gun salute might be even better.

I'll begin my commentary on that set of remarks by pointing out that the first statement contains a contradiction. It speaks of education as perfectly *conceived* but implies that that perfection is also achievable *in human experience*. Therein lies the nub of the problem I've been discussing at some length. Perfection is always *conceivable*, as I've repeatedly acknowledged, but it is not *achievable*, sad to say, save under artificially rigged conditions. In an article in the *New Yorker* the critic Adam Gopnik, writing about cookbooks, has wisely said, "Anyone who cooks knows that it is in following recipes that one first learns the anticlimax of the actual, the perpetual disappointment of the thing achieved."[2] *The anticlimax of the actual* hits the nail on the head. Its accuracy highlights the hidden flaw in the beginning of Dewey's closing remarks. Recipes hold out the promise of a perfect and intimate union between science and art.

2. Adam Gopnik, *New Yorker,* November 23, 2009, 106.

The dish when served, however, often proves disappointing, at least to the cook.

The next three of Dewey's statements offer riffs on the same theme. They reinforce the close relation between science and art with an emphasis on the special contributions of psychology and the social sciences. They also underscore the importance of education in providing a crucial service to individuals and to the society at large.

The remaining three remarks focus specifically on the role of the teacher. In an almost step-by-step exaltation they elevate that role to the point of likening the teacher to a religious leader, a prophet of the true God. Read today, Dewey's concluding salvo is almost embarrassing. It's hard to imagine any of today's educational leaders using such language. Indeed, I doubt that Dewey himself would have done so forty years on. Styles of speaking and writing, even ceremonially, change with the times.

Yet there remains something right about that final apotheosis. It expresses a sentiment that contains at least a healthy dollop of truth. Teachers do prophesy in a manner of speaking. They peer into the future in a way that their students are as yet ill equipped to do. They therefore can both warn of upcoming dangers and forecast future delights. In sum, they know a fair amount about what lies ahead, at least probabilistically and in the short run.

But does that make every teacher a prophet of the true God, as Dewey so hyperbolically proclaims? Not very likely, I'd say. It does so only if we conceive of "the true God" in Dewey's own terms.

He employs phrases like "the formation of the proper social life" and "maintenance of proper social order" to stand for the gradual realization of an earthly Shangri-la, rather like Plato's *Republic* perhaps, a heaven on earth that one day will come to resemble God's own kingdom. But such phrases, with their social-this and social-that endings, sound sadly tepid to me. They too closely resemble George Orwell's "double-talk" in *1984*. I conclude, therefore, that the strong religious language contained in the final trumpet blast of the Pedagogic Creed was rhetorical overkill. Dewey was obviously

carried away by his own enthusiasm. He too much wanted to follow
the rhetorical tradition of nineteenth-century orators by ending on
a high note.

Yet we must not let that rhetorical faux pas blind us to an even
deeper truth than the half-joke about teachers being able to prophesy. Teachers obviously are not prophets in the biblical sense. That's
clearly not how Dewey intended to portray them. Nor, despite his
use of the word "God," can education as a whole be looked on as a
kind of ersatz religion. To treat it as such borders on blasphemy.

That said, the issue of education's resemblance to religion remains open to sympathetic inspection. For even when stripped of
all exaggerated claims, education continues to share with religion
one vital characteristic. It too aims high. It too pursues perfection,
albeit more mundanely, safe to say, than the perfection traditionally
ascribed to God.

Yet here is the point: the relative height of those aspirations in
the two endeavors doesn't let us tell them apart definitively. For perfection in both cases exceeds all limits. It is always out of reach. Like
the distant horizon that separates sky and earth, it stands for a goal
that mariners fix on but never attain.

THE INFINITUDE OF PERFECTION

The infinitude of perfection sets the ultimate, unattainable standard not only for education and religion but also for science, art,
and philosophy. All five endeavors aspire to witness the unattainable, which is impossible.

Here one or two observations from Kant come in handy. In his
treatment of the transcendental problems of pure reason, Kant
points out that the object being sought "can never come before
you because it cannot be given in any possible experience."[3] He
continues,

3. Immanuel Kant, *Critique of Pure Reason*, ed. Paul Guyer and Allen W. Wood
(Cambridge: Cambridge University Press, 1998), 507, A483.

With all possible perceptions, you always remain caught up under *conditions*, whether in space or time, and you never get to the unconditioned. . . . For your object is merely in your brain and cannot be given at all outside it; hence all you have to worry about is agreement with yourself. . . . Thus the dogmatic solution is not merely uncertain but impossible. The critical solution, however, which can be completely certain, does not consider the question objectively at all, but instead asks about the foundations of the cognition in which it is grounded."[4]

What I think Kant means here is that we may never be able to reach the unconditional basis of any of our conceptions, but we are always free to criticize in a rationally acceptable manner any aspect of those conceptions that society at large now *takes* to be unconditional. Those aspects open to criticism are in a sense foundational. They are the ground on which the concept currently rests. Further on in his *Critique* he calls unconditional necessity "the true abyss" for human reason.[5] It is so, he explains, because it can't be satisfied and yet we can't rest content with that.

Is education any different foundationally from science, art, religion, and philosophy? In the finale of his Pedagogic Creed Dewey makes it seem so, but I'm not sure he's right. In fact, I'd wager he's wrong. Each of those domains of thought and creative invention offers ample opportunity for the pursuit of perfection. Judging one of them to be more caught up in that pursuit than the others seems unwise.

It remains true, however, that the pursuit of perfection is by no means limited to what goes on within those five domains. One may seek perfection in almost every human endeavor. One may try to become a perfect cook, or a perfect gardener, or even a perfect friend. All performers aspire to perfection, though some obviously

4. Ibid.
5. Ibid., 574.

try harder than others and come closer to their goal. Star athletes and musical virtuosos come immediately to mind.

Yet the perfection sought in the arts and sciences broadly speaking, which for me includes education, religion, and philosophy, seems to be of a different cast. It stands for a higher ambition than is sought in many other endeavors. What accounts for that difference? I think the answer lies hidden within Dewey's tepid talk about the proper social life, the proper social order, and the right social growth.

What remains buried in those bland phrases is the forthright recognition that the ultimate beneficiary of all five of those grand artistic and scientific efforts is humanity in general and even the world at large. The word "social" refers to a human community, a community capable of actions that are proper and right—capable, that is, of sustaining life, order, and growth among its members. Ideally that community includes not only the whole human race but everything that lives and breathes. All, in short, that depends for its sustenance on the earth's bounty.

I began this section by paraphrasing Paul Tillich's condensed version of the meaning of freedom, which he defines as "openness to norms of unconditional validity." I now can bring our discussion of that definition to a close by pointing out that the norms Tillich speaks of are always at the forefront of a community's search for perfection. They are as far as current members of that community, or at least the most authoritative among them, are willing to go at present. Until further notice, the validity of those norms is considered unconditional. Mature members of the community willingly abide by them. Younger and newer members are entreated to join the company of those already enrolled. Organized education thus becomes the community's chief means of formalizing that entreaty.

I must note, however, that the unconditional status of those norms is basically fictional. For those norms do change over time, some far more readily than others. They thus remain open to criticism, as Kant points out.

But if those norms are to be socially valuable, that criticism must be responsible. It must adhere to the rules of reason, which are themselves normative. It must also be positive as well as negative. It must defend those norms worthy of preservation while ferreting out others that need to be modified or replaced. One of the tasks of education in a democratic society is to allow for and even encourage that kind of responsible criticism from its citizens. It does so by giving students the freedom to question authority, albeit responsibly. Such freedom when properly exercised becomes the prime condition that makes both individual and social progress possible.

7

Education as a
Moral Enterprise

Two topics remain to be treated before I bring this book to a close. One is the acquaintanceship that develops between persons, especially as it occurs or fails to occur between teachers and their students. The other requires a return to the brief definition of education I came up with when I started exploring Dewey's 1938 invitation to his audience of educators. That definition, I have come to see, sorely needs an addendum. Accordingly, I shall undertake that repair. What links these two topics is that they both have to do with the moral nature of education.

MUTUAL RECOGNITION AND PERSONHOOD

At the entrance to the campus of Carroll College in Waukesha, Wisconsin, there once stood a sign that read:

CARROLL COLLEGE
Large Enough to Serve You
Small Enough to Know You

Perhaps that sign is still there. I hope it is.

I recall being struck by both the aptness and the brevity of that succinct advertisement as I drove past some years ago. "That's ex-

actly what a college should be," I thought at the time, "large enough
to serve you, yet small enough to know you. Yes sirree Bob! That
hits the nail on the head!" Well, maybe that's overdoing my reaction,
which an inborn penchant to ham things up makes me do from time
to time, but I do recall responding with considerable enthusiasm.

I since have thought long and hard about the significance of its
brief message. I now see even more clearly how important it is to be
known personally by at least a handful of those individuals who are
directly responsible for the conduct of one's formal education.

Why is that so important? Because, I now would say, being known
by someone and knowing them in return—"mutual recognition" is
what Hegel calls it[1]—is the condition of our becoming more fully
human. It is what transforms each of us from merely being human
into the kind of person we each become, with distinctive traits and
characteristics.

In his *Phenomenology of Spirit* Hegel's account of that transforma-
tion is portrayed memorably, though negatively. Through an extended tale of his own making, actually a parable, he illustrates the
crippling effect of the absence of mutual recognition in the ongo-
ing relationship between a master and his servant. Its absence leads,
ironically, to a reversal of roles. The story ends with the servant's
becoming, in effect, a master and the master's becoming in effect a
servant. But each remains deeply scarred by the sad history of their
initial relationship.

Mutual recognition and personhood. The conjoining of those
two terms reminds us that humans are not born as persons. They
become persons as they develop. They do so, moreover, largely as a
result of how others treat them.

That set of observations surely comes as no surprise. In fact it's
rather trite. We all know how important the presence of others can
be in our lives. We experience its importance daily. Yet despite its
importance, the truth it stands for is seldom at the forefront of our
thinking as we deal with others face-to-face. Perhaps that's because

1. See, for example, Georg W. F. Hegel, *Philosophy of Right*, trans. T. M. Knox (London: Oxford University Press, 1967), sec. 57.

of its triteness. It is so obvious that it escapes attention, like Poe's purloined letter. Or it could be that we fail to attend it simply because we have other things on our minds. The latter, I'd guess, is more likely.

Whatever its cause, the cost of overlooking those fundamental truths can at times be great. This is especially so within an educational context, I've come to see. It's there that so many lifelong attitudes and dispositions take root and flourish or, conversely, wither on the vine.

What are some of those attitudes and dispositions? They chiefly have to do with how we see ourselves as learners and possessors of knowledge. Other people, of course, contribute to our judgment of ourselves in those two capacities, but the most crucial judgments, at least initially, are made by teachers and other school officials. It is how they see us as learners that really counts in forming our own judgment. Moreover, family and friends almost always take their cue in such matters from what teachers and school officials have already more or less established.

The impact of those educational judgments does not stop at establishing a student's self-image as a student. It extends to other aspects of his sense of worth. The distinction between being a good student and being a good person or between a poor student and a bad person is not easily drawn. Our self-image tends to be more or less unitary. Its various components are not easily compartmentalized.

All teachers are surely aware of these rudimentary truths. They hardly need be reminded that their professional judgments of their students count for a lot. From time to time, however, they tend to overlook their potency. Why? One quick answer is that teachers often have other things on their minds beyond the psychological well-being of their students.

Teachers are not psychotherapists, not by a long shot. Nor should they try to be. Their primary task is to equip students with the skills and understanding that will allow them to function effectively in the world at large. We could say that teaching, as conventionally understood, has less to do with "forming" than with "informing."

The Priority of "Informing" over "Forming" as a Goal of Teaching
Students routinely look on their teachers as founts of knowledge.
A significant portion of the general public does so as well, seeing
teachers as in the business of passing along what they know. Many
teachers likely share that common perception, but not all do.
Some have a far less mechanical conception of their pedagogical
responsibilities.

In an essay written several years ago,[2] I tried to draw a distinction between what I called "the mimetic" and "the transformative"
traditions of teaching. (I now think I should have named the latter
"formative" rather than "transformative," a term that Webster ac-
cepts but my computer insists on flagging as misspelled.) The first
I named "mimetic," "because it gives a central place to the transmission of factual and procedural knowledge from one person to
another, through an essentially *imitative* process."[3] The second I
called "transformative" because it seeks to accomplish "a transfor-
mation of one kind or another in the person being taught—a quali-
tative change often of dramatic proportion, a metamorphosis, so to
speak."[4] The latter, I go on to say, "would include all those traits
of character and of personality most highly prized by the society at
large (aside from those having to do solely with the possession of
knowledge *per se*)."[5]

Both outlooks were called "traditions," as I further explained,
"Because each has a long and respectable history going back at least
several hundred years and possibly beyond. Also, each is more than
an intellectual argument. Each provokes feelings of partisanship and
loyalty toward a particular point of view; each also entails commitment to a set of related practices."[6]

2. Philip W. Jackson, *The Practice of Teaching* (New York: Teachers College Press,
1986), chap. 6, 115–45.
3. Ibid., 117.
4. Ibid., 120.
5. Ibid., 121.
6. Ibid, 116.

The distinction I was trying to draw is related to the one I am making here between "informing" and "forming" as pedagogical goals. The goal of "informing" bears a close resemblance to what I called the "mimetic" tradition, whereas that of "forming" resembles what I called the "transformative" tradition. Yet at present I have a slightly different take on that earlier distinction. I now see it as involving not only those teachers we encounter face-to-face but also those whose influence has been far more distant and symbolically transmitted. Let me explain.

The book the mimetic/transformative essay appears in was dedicated to eleven of my own teachers: two from elementary school, two from high school, three from college, and four from my concluding years of graduate study. After listing their names, which I won't bother to repeat here, the dedication reads, "teachers all, remembered with gratitude and affection."

What interests me now as I reflect on the relation between forming and informing, on the one hand, and the mimetic and transformative traditions, on the other, is the distinction between gratitude and affection as expressed in that dedication. I was indeed grateful to those eleven teachers for their contribution to my education, and I remain so today. But I also developed a genuine affection for each of them. I liked them as persons, and I believe they liked me. At least I know that each of them knew me rather well for a time and treated me in a very friendly manner. Their friendship affected me deeply even though its immediacy lasted for only a year or so at most. It contributed significantly to my love of education and to my decision to become an educator.

The memory of that lasting influence got me thinking about the enduring impact that other individuals have had in my life, including many I have never known personally and who have never known me. John Dewey, for example. Or Rousseau. Or Kant and Hegel. Or even that classic philosophical duo, Plato and Aristotle! They too have had a formative influence on me, for which I am indeed grateful. Yet I can't say I feel a genuine affection for any of those intellectual giants of the past. But reading their works certainly did more than merely inform me. It shaped me.

I next started thinking about the many textbooks I dutifully studied in school and college: foreign-language textbooks, mathematics textbooks, science textbooks—the list goes on and on. They too influenced my ways of thinking and acting, sometimes profoundly, as I recall, yet I don't feel particularly grateful to their authors. I can't even recall their names. I probably never noticed them in the first place.

Now what about the distinction between the mimetic and the transformative? How does that fit in here? It begins to do so, I believe, when I consider the many living teachers I've had over the course of my life in addition to those named in my book's dedication. Many of those teachers I have long forgotten. Their influence was transitory, even though it may have left me more knowledgeable and better able to do this or that. They're like the textbooks that, once read, were set aside and never consulted again. They may have served a very useful purpose at the time, but the mark they left turned out not to be personally indelible.

So the way one is affected by a teacher isn't just a question of whether that teacher was the author of a book or a living person known at first hand. Nor is it a matter of being known personally by that teacher. I'm sure many of the teachers I've forgotten once knew me personally. The real issue is my coming to identify with certain of those teachers, wanting to be like them in some way. That willingness to identify with someone else, to befriend them, so to speak, is greatly encouraged when it is reciprocal, which can happen only between living persons. That is the condition Hegel speaks of as "mutual recognition."

This line of thought brings us back to the sign in front of Carroll College and to its boast of being "large enough to serve you, yet small enough to know you." The words "large" and "small" make it sound as though the size of the college might be key to the success of that claim. Carroll College, the sign implied, is just right in size, not too large and not too small, sort of like the baby bear's not too hard and not too soft bed that Goldilocks finally fell asleep in. But is that it? Is size the key to its message? Let's think about that for a minute.

What does "large enough to serve you" mean? As applied to a college, it means having adequate physical facilities, an ample and well-trained staff and faculty, and a curriculum rich enough to offer a wide range of intellectual choices and opportunities to all who attend. All of that has to do with size, all right, but only indirectly.

What does "small enough to know you" mean? If we strip it down to its barest essentials, it hardly has to do with size at all. It simply means that at this college students will not be allowed to fall through the cracks. They will not become lost in the crowd. It means that the college's personnel, its teachers and administrators, will treat its students as individuals rather than as nameless and faceless members of an aggregation known as the "student body."

The pledge that its students will be known individually by faculty and staff constitutes a moral promise by the college authorities. It is not a vow guaranteeing that every one of its students will be known personally by every one of his teachers. That likely would be impossible. But it strongly implies that none of its students will remain completely unknown personally by all the teachers and other officials in the college. It tacitly acknowledges, in other words, that mutual recognition between persons of low and high status is a high priority and an essential condition for human flourishing. That's Hegel's point as well.

Most of us can never be recognized by the most renowned of our intellectual and spiritual progenitors. We can only admire them from afar by reading their works or reveling in the enjoyment of their artistic creations. That admiration is definitely not mutual.

Yet we can be led to that admiration by others, some of whom *do* take an interest in us personally. Among the latter, those who serve as our teachers in a formal sense constitute an extremely influential group. They are the ones we most fondly remember when reminiscing about our schooldays. We who teach should never lose sight of that potential aspect of our influence.

On the Primacy of Love in Teaching and Learning
I earlier noted that those teachers to whom I dedicated my book contributed significantly to my love of education and to my

decision to become an educator. I also mentioned that I felt not only gratitude but genuine affection toward them. To introduce words like "love" and "affection" into a discussion aimed at uncovering the essence of education may seem a bit odd at first. Those terms may strike some readers as being out of place in such a context. A bit too mushy perhaps.

Yet we readily use such language when talking informally about educational matters. When reminiscing we commonly say things like "I loved dear old Miss What's-her-name, my third-grade teacher" or, rather more impersonally, "I love studying history, don't you?" Many of us as we age may one day find ourselves saying, as I once did, "I love education. Period."

But when we employ the word "love" that casually, aren't we merely using it as a figure of speech, without serious intent? After all, we also say things like "I love chocolate ice cream" or "I love the New York Yankees." But we don't really mean we *love* those things, do we?

I'm not so sure. I think we mean that we feel close to those objects toward which we profess love. We identify with them in some sense. We possess them. They become "ours," our favored this or that. In that sense, therefore, these forms of attachment reduce the separation between subject and object. They bring the two closer together, which is the principal goal of education.

How important are such expressions of affection in an educational context? What do they add to our conceptual understanding of education? I believe they add a lot. They help us see that under ideal conditions the emotion of love in one or another of its many forms touches on all the components of our educational experience. It attaches to persons, to the material being studied, and to the totality of the experience itself. Moreover, it does so, or can do so, for teachers and students alike. Without those attachments in one form or another, education loses much of its appeal. It becomes stripped of its ultimate meaning.

At the same time, it is important to recognize that feelings akin to love can also be differentially attached to education's components. Moreover, negative emotions may be present as well. A student may love to study a particular school subject, for example, but dislike the person then teaching it. Conversely, the same student may be very fond of an individual teacher but dislike having to study the assigned material. The combinations and permutations of those differential likings and dislikings are of course extremely varied. The same hold true for teachers' preferences.

Teachers obviously not only can feel attached to individual students, they can have similar feelings, both positive and negative, toward other aspects of their work. Partitioned into the barest of categories, an individual teacher can love primarily *who* she is teaching, *what* she is teaching, or *how* she is teaching. Ideally, of course, she loves all three with equal fervor, but that happy arrangement needn't always hold. She may love one of those three components markedly more than the other two. Those differences will affect the kind of teacher she chooses to become.

The teacher who prefers to work with very young children, for example, will likely wind up teaching in a nursery school or kindergarten. The one whose love of a particular school subject is intense will naturally aspire to teach in a high school or college. The teacher who especially enjoys the give-and-take of classroom life and who savors the challenge of working with many kinds of students may jump at the chance to work in a self-contained classroom in a public elementary school or even in a multigrade setting such as was common in the one-room school, now all but extinct. What is wanted, of course, are teachers whose love of teaching in all its aspects is reasonably high. That may not always be achievable, but it is a standard to work for.

All of this boils down to the realization that love plays a vital role in education for students and teachers alike. It is the glue that holds things together, that makes them cohere. This says to teachers that if teaching cannot be performed lovingly in some important sense that brings the teacher a deep contentment, it probably shouldn't be performed at all. The rule is simple: If you love nothing about teaching, get out of it.

This brings us to what might be called education's bottom line, which is the conclusion that education, au fond, is a moral enterprise.

It is so because it aims at improvement. It seeks to make everyone it touches, teachers as well as students, better than they are now. Viewed globally, it tries to leave the world a better place. Its task is endless for the simple reason that each new generation of humans needs to be educated. But it is also endless because each new generation is free to build on, to "rectify and expand," as Dewey might put it, the accomplishments of generations past.

A SHORT DEFINITION OF EDUCATION RECONSIDERED

You will recall that when I first began puzzling over Dewey's advice at the close of *Experience and Education* I decided he was asking his audience to come up with a fresh definition of education, one brief enough to remember and put to use. Accordingly, I produced a nine-word definition of my own. Education, I decided, was nothing more and nothing less than *a socially facilitated process of cultural transmission*.

I soon grew dissatisfied with that definition, as you will also recall. I came to see that there was far more to education than those few words allowed. I trust that most of you readily agree and probably came to that conclusion long before I did.

More important, I decided early on that Dewey must have been asking his audience to do something far more ambitious than come up with a brief definition. That's the point where the adventure outlined in this book truly got under way.

That adventure has taken us in several directions, some of them unexpected at the start. We have penetrated at least the outskirts, if not the dark netherworld, of German idealism, where Dewey began his own philosophical quest as a young man. Most of all, we have come to see that Dewey was asking his 1938 audience not just to *define* education as one might define a single word but to say something definitive about its *essence*, about what it is au fond. Aided by the writings of Kant, Hegel, and others, we have further come to see that education's essence is by no means the same as its existence. Its essence is invisible; it must be inferred. Its existence consists of what can be seen and heard as education is translated into action.

Distinguishing between essence and existence is important because translating education into action inevitably falls short. Its essence, which exists solely as an ideal, is never fully realized. Indeed,
education's ideal itself changes over time, though at a far more glacial
pace than the components of its existence. Several of those components come as close to being immutable as human understanding,
historically and culturally conditioned, can make them.

Among its most immutable components, as I trust we will now
agree, are the two I started out with in my nine-word definition. To
repeat, education is first of all a socially facilitated process. Second,
that process is basically one of cultural transmission. What those
two components imply is, first, that education calls for social coop-
eration. It is not something that happens naturally or automatically.
It entails enacting a social obligation that each generation owes to
the next. Second, it involves transmitting something that is considered valuable by those in charge of the operation. That transmission
takes time. It does not happen overnight. It requires work and effort
from everyone involved.

Those two components of education's essence may sound too
obvious to mention, but from them flow a host of unexpected con-
sequences, as we have seen. Examining their significance more fully,
we have also come to see that education is fundamentally a moral
enterprise. Its goal is to effect beneficial changes in humans, not just
in what they know and can do but, more important, in their character and personality, in the kind of persons they become. Moreover,
the beneficiaries of that process are not just the individuals being
served but also the society at large. Ultimately, the world in general
stands to benefit from such an effort.

Is that too lofty a take on what might be called education's essence? Possibly so. It begins to sound a bit like Dewey's impassioned
outburst at the end of his Pedagogic Creed. The comparison should
give us pause, but it should hardly deter us from probing ever more
deeply into education's essence. That deeper and fuller appreciation
of education's moral task must simply be added to whatever rough-
and-ready definition of the term may have served us at the start. At
the same time, our definition must be kept relatively brief. Only

then will it remain lodged in memory, where it stands ever ready for repeated use.

There is this about it as well: that extended definition must be ours personally. It can't just be what Dewey or Hegel or Kant or anyone else happens to think. It has to be a subjective truth for each of us, as I explained in chapter 3. That doesn't mean it can't incorporate the words of others, or even be a full-blown copy of someone else's conclusion. But it has to be a definition that each of us *takes to be true* in a very personal sense. It also should be expandable. Each of us, in other words, might use such a statement as a launching pad for the fuller articulation of our own pedagogical creed.

I now think that's what Dewey was inviting his audience to do. He was asking each of them to begin hammering out his own pedagogical creed, starting perhaps with a crude definition of education and moving on from there. What happens when someone tries to do that? Will such an effort lead to acceptance of Dewey's idea of what education is all about? Maybe so, but maybe not. The ultimate destination of such a private line of thought always remains to be seen.

So here is my own revised definition of education, a bit longer than the one I started with but still brief. You are urged to alter it as you see fit or, if you prefer, to reject it completely and begin fresh.

> Education is a socially facilitated process of cultural transmission whose explicit goal is to effect an enduring change for the better in the character and psychological well-being (the personhood) of its recipients and, by indirection, in their broader social environment, which ultimately extends to the world at large.

Has the exercise of arriving at that expanded definition been worth the effort? I would say yes, definitely, but in the end that judgment rests with each one of my readers. What I hope each of you will have gained most from our shared journey is a firm conviction (or at least a firmer one) that there are no final answers to the questions Dewey posed back in 1938. There are only attempts at such answers, all of them imperfect.

Yet all such attempts edify in one way or another. Those of us who undertake them are led to the edge of our current understanding and possibly a few steps beyond. In venturing to take those few extra steps we leave empiricism behind and enter the domain of metaphysics, or of what both Kant and Hegel often refer to as speculative or dialectical thought. Additionally, in doing so we overstep, at least for a time, the boundaries of Dewey's experience-based pragmatism.

That being the case, perhaps Kant, rather than Dewey, should be allowed to offer a final word of encouragement to all who may choose to follow a path similar to the one my readers and I have traversed in these pages. In his *Critique of Pure Reason* Kant says this in defense of speculative thought: "Mere honesty requires that a reflective and inquiring being should devote certain times solely to testing its own reason . . . letting the propositions and counter-propositions . . . come forward to defend themselves before a jury drawn from their own estate (namely the estate of fallible human beings)."[7] With respect to the nosegay of questions Dewey tossed to his Kappa Delta Pi audience, the jury Kant alludes to is definitely still out. And well it should be. For when it comes to conceptual truths the ultimate jury resides within each of us. That's what a proper education, faithfully pursued, helps us understand.

In sum, to rethink education at some length, as we have done together here, is to reaffirm the moral importance of the enterprise, thereby rededicating ourselves to its service without pausing to acknowledge, till now, that when all is said and done, that rededication is exactly the task we have been jointly, albeit unwittingly, engaged in. It becomes so each time we turn our thoughts in the direction of education pure and simple.

7. Immanuel Kant, *Critique of Pure Reason*, ed. Paul Guyer and Allen W. Wood (Cambridge: Cambridge University Press, 1998), 503, A476/B504.

Further Reading

Because this book was not written for an audience of professional philosophers, or even amateur ones for that matter, a fair number of readers may be relatively unacquainted with the writings of the three philosophers—Dewey, Kant, and Hegel—whose ideas figure most prominently in its pages. Some may wish to know more not only about those three men and their ideas, but also about the broader philosophical context of their work. Living in the computer age, as we do, the easy way to satisfy that desire would be to turn on one's PC or Mac and tap into Google and Wikipedia, where a deluge of information awaits. I was tempted to take that route myself in preparing these suggestions for further reading, but I decided on an approach more in keeping, I felt, with the spirit of this book. I chose to be far more personal than the anonymous Google or Wikipedia can ever be. The following compilation, therefore, which possibly constitutes overkill fully as much as the torrent provided by a computer, cites only those sources that I have drawn on and profited from in writing this book and in the years of study that preceded the actual writing. It has four sections: one each for Dewey, Kant, and Hegel and one that treats the broader philosophical background of their work and all of modernity. With one or two exceptions, I own each of the books I'll mention. They cram the shelves of my study and overflow them. The suggestions culled from those

crowded shelves are limited in scope, however. They are addressed
principally to those who are starting almost from scratch to explore
the intellectual terrain that begins just beyond the final pages of this
book. More advanced readers who chance to peruse these recommendations may also find a few of its citations unfamiliar and worthy of further exploration.

DEWEY

Dewey's *Collected Works* in seventeen volumes, edited by Jo Ann
Boydston, is published by Southern Illinois University Press. Each
volume begins with a helpful introductory essay written by a Dewey
scholar. The collection as a whole is especially valuable in that, in
addition to all of Dewey's books, it contains the many essays and re-
views he wrote throughout his long life. Dewey was a prolific writer,
as those seventeen volumes attest, and many of his shorter pieces are
just as fascinating and informative as most of his longer and better-
known works. The *Collected Works* are available in most university
libraries. They also can be purchased online or in bookstores, singly
in paperback or the entire set on a single CD. Many of Dewey's major works can also be found in secondhand bookstores.

A good introduction to Dewey's educational ideas is contained in
two small books, *The School and Society* and *The Child and the Curriculum*, written while Dewey was head of the newly established Laboratory School at the University of Chicago. They were published
separately but are currently available in a single volume published by
the University of Chicago Press. Dewey's most noteworthy book on
education, but unfortunately not his most widely read, is *Democracy
and Education*, published in 1916. *How We Think: A Restatement of the
Relation of Reflective Thinking to the Educative Process* was written for
teachers and was initially published in 1909. A revised and enlarged
edition came out in 1933 and is by far superior to the original. A sixti-
eth anniversary reissue of *Experience and Education* was published by
Kappa Delta Pi in 1998. A handy collection of Dewey's briefer educational writings, titled *Dewey on Education* and introduced by Martin S. Dworkin, was published by Teachers College Press in 1959 and

is still in print. Another useful collection is *John Dewey on Education: Selected Writings*, edited by Reginald D. Archambault.

In addition to his writings on education, a number of Dewey's other books should certainly be of interest to educational practitioners. *Art as Experience, Human Nature and Conduct, Experience and Nature, The Quest for Certainty, Reconstruction in Philosophy, A Common Faith*, and *The Public and Its Problems* are ones that come most readily to mind. They all are of enduring value. The order they're read in does not matter particularly, though I'd recommend starting with *Art as Experience*, since it treats a topic that bears directly on the central thesis of this book.

The secondary literature on Dewey's life and works is also voluminous. There is even a separate guide to that literature titled *Works about John Dewey: 1886–1995*, compiled and edited by Barbara Levine. Another valuable compilation, *Dewey and His Critics*, is edited by Sidney Morgenbesser, who was one of Dewey's younger colleagues at Columbia University. Biographical studies include George Dykhuizen's *The Life and Mind of John Dewey*, Stephen Rockefeller's *John Dewey: Religious Faith and Democratic Humanism*, Jay Martin's *The Education of John Dewey*, Robert B. Westbrook's *John Dewey and American Democracy*, Alan Ryan's *John Dewey and the High Tide of American Liberalism*, and Thomas C. Dalton's *Becoming John Dewey*. All are worth reading, but the one that offers the most intimate portrayal of Dewey's personal life, which may be of special interest to newcomers, is probably Martin's *Education of John Dewey*.

Books that treat Dewey's thought in general are far too numerous to list in full. An almost random sampling of representative volumes, alphabetically arranged, would include Thomas Alexander, *John Dewey's Theory of Art, Experience, and Nature*; James Campbell, *Understanding John Dewey*; Michael Eldridge, *Transforming Experience: John Dewey's Cultural Instrumentalism*; Steven M. Fishman and Lucille McCarthy, *John Dewey and the Philosophy and Practice of Hope*; Jim Garrison, *Dewey and Eros: Wisdom and Desire in the Art of Teaching*; George Geiger, *John Dewey in Perspective*; James A. Good, *A Search for Unity in Diversity: The "Permanent Hegelian Deposit" in the*

Philosophy of John Dewey; James Gouinlick, *John Dewey's Philosophy of Value*; David Granger, *John Dewey, Robert Pirsig, and the Art of Living*; Larry Hickman, *John Dewey's Pragmatic Technology*; Philip W. Jackson, *John Dewey and the Lessons of Art* and *John Dewey and the Philosopher's Task*; Victor Kestenbaum, *The Grace and Severity of the Ideal: John Dewey and the Transcendent*; Daniel F. Rice, *Reinhold Niebuhr and John Dewey: An American Odyssey*; and R. W. Sleeper, *The Necessity of Pragmatism: John Dewey's Conception of Philosophy*. I can think of no sensible way to guide readers intelligibly through that maze of books. Setting aside my own two contributions to the list, whose quality I cannot properly comment on, all are written by competent and well-qualified authors, each looking at Dewey's writings from a slightly different angle. The best advice I can give is to let each book's title and subtitle determine its immediate appeal.

The same is true of collections of essays dealing with one or another aspect of Dewey's work. They too are numerous, with a new volume appearing almost annually of late, or so it seems. Among those gracing a corner of my study at present are *In Dewey's Wake: Unfinished Work of Pragmatic Reconstruction*, edited by William J. Gavin; *The New Scholarship on Dewey*, edited by Jim Garrison; *John Dewey and Our Educational Prospect: A Critical Engagement with Dewey's Democracy and Education*, edited by David T. Hansen; *Dewey Reconfigured: Essays on Deweyan Pragmatism*, edited by Casey Haskins and David I. Seiple; *Reading Dewey: Interpretations for a Postmodern Generation*, edited by Larry Hickman; and *John Dewey Reconsidered*, edited by R. S. Peters. They are all worth dipping into and even perusing at some length as a way of becoming acquainted with the range and depth of Dewey scholarship.

For a peek at an aspect of Dewey's personal life that seldom gets discussed, take a look at *The Poems of John Dewey*, edited by Jo Ann Boydston. Dewey was a closet poet during an important decade of his life. Most of his poems are not very good, in my opinion, but the story behind their writing and their later discovery is fascinating.

The trick in reading Dewey (or any philosopher, for that matter) is to read him slowly. Dewey was not a great writer stylistically. Many have remarked on the occasional opacity of his prose. But neither was he a careless writer. He customarily weighed his words. Consequently, he generally meant what he said, a presumption I have tried to act on in writing this book. His writings therefore deserve respect. Like most philosophical works, they almost always repay slow and careful reading.

KANT

Kant's trio of critiques constitute his major contribution to philosophy. Sequentially, they are *Critique of Pure Reason*, *Critique of Practical Reason*, and *Critique of the Power of Judgment*. The first was published in 1781 and the third in 1790. All three are considered masterpieces, although they are not easy reading. The Princeton philosopher Walter Kaufmann once called Kant's first *Critique* "one of the worst-written great books of all time."[1] The first deals principally with reason alone, the second with matters of morality, and the third with questions of aesthetics. But they are probably not books that a beginner should tackle without preparation and possibly not before reading some less demanding works by Kant himself.

A good way to begin, in my opinion, is with some introductory material that opens the door to Kant's work as a whole. Many such books are available, but I recommend taking a look at either Stephan Körner's *Kant*, Roger Scruton's *Kant*, Allen Wood's *Kant*, or possibly all three. Scruton's is the briefest and Wood's the most up-to-date, but all three are introductory in nature and quite helpful as stepping-stones to the door of Kant's inner sanctum. Another introduction, which itself has become a classic, is Ernst Cassirer's *Kant's Life and Thought*. It is longer and far more biographical than the three I have mentioned, but it is certainly well worth reading at some point in one's exploration of Kant's many contributions to human understanding.

Works by Kant himself that are rather less demanding than his three *Critiques* include his *Prolegomena to Any Future Metaphysics*, his

1. Walter Kaufmann, *Critique of Religion and Philosophy* (Princeton, NJ: Princeton University Press, 1978), 7.

Groundwork of the Metaphysics of Morals, his *Religion within the Limits of Reason Alone*, and his *Logic*. All those books have won the respect of scholars worldwide and are commonly studied independently in colleges and universities. The *Prolegomena* is probably the one to begin with, for many consider it the best of all introductions to the *Critique of Pure Reason*. A useful collection of Kant's essays, titled *Religion and Rational Theology*, was translated and edited by Allen Wood and George di Giovanni.

Two of the most prolific and senior Anglophone commentators on Kant's work are Henry Allison and Paul Guyer. Allison's books on Kant include *Idealism and Freedom*, *Kant's Theory of Taste*, *Kant's Theory of Freedom*, and *Kant's Transcendental Idealism*. The last-named is now in its second edition. Guyer's books on Kant include *Kant and the Experience of Freedom*, *Kant on Freedom, Law, and Happiness*, and *Kant and the Claims of Taste*. He has also edited *The Cambridge Companion to Kant*, which contains many helpful essays. The books of both those commentators are worth careful study.

Two of the most highly respected commentators on Kant, though less prolific than Allison and Guyer, are Christine Korsgaard and Karl Ameriks. Korsgaard's *Creating the Kingdom of Ends* deserves special attention, even by neophytes, as does Ameriks's *Interpreting Kant's Critiques*.

HEGEL

Hegel's principal writings, leaving aside his juvenilia and his many lectures (which I shall return to presently), are essentially four. Sequentially, they are the *Phenomenology of Spirit* (1806), the *Science of Logic* (1812–16), the *Encyclopedia of the Philosophical Sciences* (1817), and the *Elements of the Philosophy of Right* (1820). The *Phenomenology* is the one to read first. It is eminently readable and sets the stage for all the others. I would follow that with the *Encyclopedia*, for it has three parts: *Logic*, *Philosophy of Mind*, and *Philosophy of Nature* (listed separately in the bibliography), the first of which is much briefer and somewhat easier going than the *Science of Logic*. I would temporarily overlook the *Philosophy of Nature*, for it is the most contested and tedious of the three parts and can be read later if desired. I then would move on to the *Philosophy of Right* before tackling the *Science of Logic* head-on. Readers who finally get around to that daunting task will be greatly helped by Stephen Houlgate's *The Opening of Hegel's "Logic": From Being to Infinity*.

Hegel's juvenilia are principally available in English in his *Early Theological Writings*. His many lectures fill several volumes. The most easily readable and probably most interesting to educators are his *Introductory Lectures on Aesthetics* and *On Art, Religion, and the History of Philosophy: Introductory Lectures*. Fuller versions of his lectures on *Aesthetics* (two volumes), *Philosophy of Religion* (one-volume version), and *History of Philosophy* (three volumes) are also available. Those whose acquaintance with Hegel's writings turns out to be anything like as richly rewarding as my own will one day want to read them all.

The most recent and readily available biography of Hegel is probably Terry Pinkard's *Hegel: A Biography*. Although Pinkard's *Biography* is good and should be read by all serious students of Hegel, a far more richly detailed account of Hegel's intellectual development is contained in H. S. Harris's monumental *Hegel's Development: Toward the Sunlight*, and *Hegel's Development: Night Thoughts*, along with his subsequent two-volume opus, *Hegel's Ladder*, volume 1, *The Pilgrimage of Reason*, and *Hegel's Ladder*, volume 2, *The Odyssey of Spirit*. The level of scholarship and the painstaking detail of Harris's work are nothing short of breathtaking.

Readers who choose to start by reading Hegel's *Phenomenology*, as I recommended, will be greatly aided by Quentin Lauer's *A Reading of Hegel's "Phenomenology of Spirit"* and by Yirmiyahu Yovel's *Hegel's Preface to the "Phenomenology of Spirit."* Both are highly readable introductions to that work. Terry Pinkard's *Hegel's Phenomenology*, Jean Hyppolite's *Genesis and Structure of Hegel's "Phenomenology of Spirit,"* Robert Solomon's *In the Spirit of Hegel*, Merold Westphal's *History and Truth in Hegel's "Phenomenology,"* and Michael Forster's *Hegel's Idea of a Phenomenology of Spirit* provide a somewhat fuller treatment of that seminal volume.

Valuable commentary on Hegel's work in general is to be found in Stephen Houlgate's *An Introduction to Hegel: Freedom, Truth, and*

History, Frederick Beiser's *Hegel*, M. J. Inwood's *Hegel*, and Charles Taylor's *Hegel*. Taylor's shorter work *Hegel and Modern Society* is also well worth reading. The briefest overview I know is Peter Singer's *Hegel*. Hegel's religious ideas are treated in some detail in Quentin Lauer's *Hegel's Concept of God* and in Emil Fackenheim's *The Religious Dimension in Hegel's Thought*. Yirmiyahu Yovel in his *Dark Riddle: Hegel, Nietzsche, and the Jews* treats the image of Judaism in the work of Hegel and Nietzsche. Hegel's political philosophy is fruitfully examined in Paul Franco's *Hegel's Philosophy of Freedom*. Michael Forster's *Hegel and Skepticism* treats the different forms of skepticism, classical and modern, to be found in Hegel's writings. Useful single-author essays on various aspects of Hegel's work appear in Quentin Lauer's *Essays in Hegelian Dialectic* and in Hans-Georg Gadamer's *Hegel's Dialectic: Five Hermeneutical Studies*. Collections of essays by various authors appear in *Hegel: A Collection of Critical Essays*, compiled by Alisdair MacIntyre; in *The Cambridge Companion to Hegel*, edited by Fredrick C. Beiser; and in *Hegel and the Arts* and *Hegel and the Philosophy of Nature*, both edited by Stephen Houlgate.

Worthy of special note is Walter Kaufmann's *Hegel: A Reinterpretation*. It is now out of print, so if you ever find it in a used bookstore, grab it. It's one of the best-written treatments of Hegel's entire life and works that I have read, though it is quite polemical in spots. For example, Kaufmann sees Hegel as being much closer to Goethe than to Kant. He also sees him as ruining his writing by trying to imitate Kant's style. You may not wind up agreeing with the book's opinions about Hegel throughout, but it's still a delight to read.

An especially penetrating study of Hegel's philosophy that has only recently appeared is Robert Pippin's *Hegel's Practical Philosophy*. For readers seeking the very latest in top-quality Hegelian scholarship, Pippin's book is outstanding.

THE BROADER PHILOSOPHICAL BACKGROUND

The broader philosophical background of the writings of Dewey, Kant, and Hegel actually extends to all of Western philosophy from the Greeks forward. Therefore any book on the history of Western philosophy will certainly help fill in that background, save perhaps *A History of Western Philosophy* by Bertrand Russell, who tends to undervalue the contributions of all three of the philosophers I have drawn on most heavily. The possibilities that remain for filling in that historical background are too numerous to begin to list. For me, however, that history, which culminates in the emergence of what we now call *modernism*, comes to a head in Germany near the end of the eighteenth century and the early decades of the nineteenth. It was then that what was to become known as German idealism ascended the night sky like a rocket whose glare illuminated the landscape of philosophical thought not only in Germany but worldwide. That glare, in my opinion, still lights the way forward for many of today's philosophers. Accordingly, the references that follow are very few in number and limited in scope. They call attention to a mere handful of books that seek to deepen our understanding of that brief phase of philosophical history whose effects continue to reverberate today.

Two of the best overviews of that history, in my opinion, are Terry Pinkard's *German Philosophy, 1760–1860*, and Frederick C. Beiser's *German Idealism: The Struggle against Subjectivism, 1781–1801*. They are both ambitious books that merit careful study, as do Robert Pippin's *Idealism as Modernism* and his *Modernism as a Philosophical Problem*. Beiser's *The Romantic Imperative: The Concept of Early German Romanticism* treats the aesthetic offshoot of German idealism in a most illuminating way. Russell B. Goodman's *American Philosophy and the Romantic Tradition* brings the story of the interconnection of romanticism and philosophy to the shores of America. Goodman, incidentally, devotes a separate chapter to Dewey and the romantic tradition that is especially worth reading.

Readers wanting to probe even deeper into such matters might wish to examine Karl Löwith's *From Hegel to Nietzsche: The Revolution in Nineteenth-Century Thought*, Leszek Kolakowski's *Modernity on Endless Trial*, and Dieter Henrich's *Between Kant and Hegel: Lectures on German Idealism*. Those wanting to read the original texts of some of the exchanges between the philosophers of Kant and Hegel's day should turn to George di Giovanni and H. S. Harris's *Between Kant and Hegel: Texts in the Development of Post-Kantian Idealism.*

Finally, for those readers who are not daunted by the prospect of reading a three-volume work in theology, I strongly recommend including in their foray into transcendental metaphysics a thorough examination of Paul Tillich's *Systematic Theology.* Tillich's monumental work draws together philosophy, psychology, and religious thought in a way that highlights the intellectual struggles that led to the flowering of German idealism. Walter Kaufmann, incidentally, in his *Critique of Religion and Philosophy*, severely criticizes Tillich, as he does a number of other prominent theologians, from Saint Thomas Aquinas forward. In short, Kaufmann has little time for theologians of any kind. His reasoning on that score is certainly worthy of attention. But whether theologically inclined or not, readers who care deeply enough about the concept of education to be willing to rethink it from the ground up from time to time have no choice, as I see it, but to wrestle with those same esoteric matters of soul and spirit that through the ages have troubled both philosophers and theologians—along with artists, moralists, and scholars in general, I might add. Many of those same questions continue to trouble thoughtful folks today.

This concludes my recommendations for further reading. I hope the suggestions prove helpful. Beyond that, I sincerely hope that you have in the main found this book worth perusing. Whatever your final judgment, however, I thank you all for the time you have spent reading these pages.

Bibliography

Alexander, Thomas M. *John Dewey's Theory of Art, Experience, and Nature*. Albany: State University of New York Press, 1987.

Allison, Henry E. *Idealism and Freedom*. New York: Cambridge University Press, 1996.

———. *Kant's Theory of Freedom*. New York: Cambridge University Press, 1990.

———. *Kant's Theory of Taste*. New York: Cambridge University Press, 2001.

———. *Kant's Transcendental Idealism*. Rev. ed. New Haven, CT: Yale University Press, 2004.

Ameriks, Karl. *Interpreting Kant's Critiques*. Oxford: Clarendon Press, 2003.

Beiser, Frederick. *German Idealism: The Struggle against Subjectivism, 1781–1801*. Cambridge, MA: Harvard University Press, 2002.

———. *Hegel*. New York: Routledge, 2005.

———. *The Romantic Imperative: The Concept of Early German Romanticism*. Cambridge, MA: Harvard University Press, 2003.

Brandom, Robert B. *Tales of the Mighty Dead: Historical Essays in the Metaphysics of Intentionality*. Cambridge, MA: Harvard University Press, 2002.

The Cambridge Companion to Hegel. Edited by Fredrick C. Beiser. Cambridge: Cambridge University Press, 1993.

The Cambridge Companion to Kant. Edited by Paul Guyer. Cambridge: Cambridge University Press, 1992.

Campbell, James. *Understanding John Dewey*. Chicago: Open Court Press, 1995.

Cassirer, Ernst. *Kant's Life and Thought*. New Haven, CT: Yale University Press, 1981.

Dalton, Thomas C. *Becoming John Dewey: Dilemmas of a Philosopher and Naturalist*. Bloomington: Indiana University Press, 2002.

Dewey, John. *Art as Experience*. New York: Capricorn Books, 1934.

———. *The Child and the Curriculum*. Chicago: University of Chicago Press, 1902.

———. *Collected Works*. Edited by Jo Ann Boydston. Carbondale: Southern Illinois University Press, 1969–91.

———. *A Common Faith*. New Haven, CT: Yale University Press, 1934.

———. *Democracy and Education*. New York: Macmillan, 1916.

———. *Dewey on Education*. Introduction and notes by Martin S. Dworkin. New York: Teachers College Press, 1959.

———. *Experience and Education*. New York: Collier Books, 1938.

———. *Experience and Education*. West Lafayette, IN: Kappa Delta Pi, 1998.

———. *Experience and Nature*. New York: Dover, 1958.

———. *How We Think*. New York: Prometheus Books, 1991.

———. *How We Think: A Restatement of the Relation of Reflective Thinking to the Educative Process*. Boston: D. C. Heath, 1933.

———. *Human Nature and Conduct: An Introduction to Social Psychology*. New York: Modern Library, 1922.

———. *John Dewey on Education: Selected Writings*. Edited by Reginald D. Archambault. New York: Modern Library, 1964.

———. *The Poems of John Dewey*, edited by Jo Ann Boydston. Carbondale: Southern Illinois University Press, 1977.

———. *The Public and Its Problems*. New York: Henry Holt, 1927.

———. *The Quest for Certainty*. New York: G. P. Putnam's Sons, 1929.

———. *Reconstruction in Philosophy*. Enl. ed. Boston: Beacon Press, 1948.

———. *The School and Society*. Chicago: University of Chicago Press, 1900.

———. *"The School and Society"; and, "The Child and the Curriculum."* Expanded ed., introduction by Philip W. Jackson. Chicago: University of Chicago Press, 1990.

Di Giovanni, George, and H. S. Harris, eds. *Between Kant and Hegel: Texts in the Development of Post-Kantian Idealism*. Indianapolis: Hackett, 2000.

Dworkin, Martin S., ed. *Dewey on Education: Selections*. New York: Teachers College Press, 1959.

Dykhuizen, George. *The Life and Mind of John Dewey*. Carbondale: Southern Illinois University Press, 1973.

Eldridge, Michael. *Transforming Experience: John Dewey's Cultural Instrumentalism*. Nashville, TN: Vanderbilt University Press, 1998.

Fackenheim, Emil. *The Religious Dimension in Hegel's Thought*. Bloomington: Indiana University Press, 1967.

Fishman, Steven M., and Lucille McCarthy. *John Dewey and the Philosophy and Practice of Hope*. Urbana: University of Illinois Press, 2007.

Forster, Michael N. *Hegel and Skepticism*. Cambridge, MA: Harvard University Press, 1989.

———. *Hegel's Idea of a Phenomenology of Spirit*. Chicago: University of Chicago Press, 1998.

Franco, Paul. *Hegel's Philosophy of Freedom*. New Haven, CT: Yale University Press, 1999.

Gadamer, Hans-Georg. *Hegel's Dialectic: Five Hermeneutical Studies*. New Haven, CT: Yale University Press, 1976.

Garrison, Jim. *Dewey and Eros: Wisdom and Desire in the Art of Teaching*. New York: Teachers College Press, 1997.

———, ed. *The New Scholarship on Dewey*. Dordrecht: Kluwer Academic Publishers, 1995.

Gavin, William J., ed. *In Dewey's Wake: Unfinished Work of Pragmatic Reconstruction*. Albany: State University of New York Press, 2003.

Geiger, George R. *John Dewey in Perspective*. New York: McGraw-Hill, 1958.

Good, James. *A Search for Unity in Diversity: The "Permanent Hegelian Deposit" in the Philosophy of John Dewey*. Lanham, MD: Lexington Books, 2006.

Goodman, Russell B. *American Philosophy and the Romantic Tradition*. New York: Cambridge University Press, 1990.

Gouinlick, James. *John Dewey's Philosophy of Value*. New York: Humanities Press, 1972.

Granger, David A. *John Dewey, Robert Pirsig, and the Art of Living*. New York: Palgrave, 2006.

Guyer, Paul. *Kant and the Claims of Taste*. New York: Cambridge University Press, 1997.

———. *Kant and the Experience of Freedom*. Cambridge: Cambridge University Press, 1996.

———. *Kant on Freedom, Law, and Happiness*. New York: Cambridge University Press, 2000.

Hansen, David T., ed. *John Dewey and Our Educational Prospect: A Critical Engagement with Dewey's Democracy and Education*. Albany: State University of New York Press, 2006.

Hardimon, Michael O. *Hegel's Social Philosophy: The Project of Reconciliation*. Cambridge: Cambridge University Press, 1994.

Harris, H. S. *Hegel: Phenomenology and System*. Indianapolis: Hackett, 1995.

———. *Hegel's Development: Night Thoughts*. Oxford: Clarendon Press, 1983.

———. *Hegel's Development: Toward the Sunlight*. Oxford: Clarendon Press, 1972.

————. *Hegel's Ladder*. Vol. 1, *The Pilgrimage of Reason*. Indianapolis: Hackett, 1997.

————. *Hegel's Ladder*. Vol. 2, *The Odyssey of Spirit*. Indianapolis: Hackett, 1997.

Haskins, Casey, and David I. Seiple, eds. *Dewey Reconfigured: Essays on Deweyan Pragmatism*. Albany: State University of New York Press, 1999.

Hegel, Georg W. F. *Aesthetics: Lectures on Fine Art*. Translated by T. M. Knox. Oxford: Clarendon Press, 1998.

————. *Early Theological Writings*. Translated by T. M. Knox and Richard Kroner. Philadelphia: University of Pennsylvania Press, 1975.

————. *Elements of the Philosophy of Right*. Cambridge: Cambridge University Press, 1991.

————. *Hegel's Logic*. Being Part One of the *Encyclopedia of the Philosophical Sciences* (1830). Translated by William Wallace. Oxford: Oxford University Press, 1975.

————. *Hegel's Philosophy of Mind*. Being Part Three of the *Encyclopedia of the Philosophical Sciences* (1830). Translated by A. V. Miller. Oxford: Oxford University Press, 1971.

————. *Hegel's Philosophy of Nature*. Being Part Two of the *Encyclopedia of the Philosophical Sciences* (1830). Translated by A. V. Miller. Oxford: Oxford University Press, 1970.

————. *Introductory Lectures on Aesthetics*. Translated by Bernard Bosanquet, edited by Michael Inwood. London: Penguin Books, 1993.

————. *Lectures on the History of Philosophy*. Vol. 1, *Greek Philosophy to Plato*. Translated by E. S. Haldane. Lincoln: University of Nebraska Press, 1995.

————. *Lectures on the History of Philosophy*. Vol. 2, *Plato and the Platonists*. Translated by E. S. Haldane and Frances H. Simson. Lincoln: University of Nebraska Press, 1995.

————. *Lectures on the History of Philosophy*. Vol. 3, *Medieval and Modern Philosophy*. Translated by E. S. Haldane and Frances H. Simson. Lincoln: University of Nebraska Press, 1995.

————. *Lectures on the Philosophy of Religion*. Edited by Peter C. Hodgson. Berkeley: University of California Press, 1988.

————. *Lectures on the Philosophy of World History: Introduction*. Cambridge: Cambridge University Press, 1975.

————. *On Art, Religion, and the Philosophy of History: Introductory Lectures*. Edited by J. Glenn Gray. Indianapolis: Hackett, 1997.

————. *Phenomenology of Spirit*. Translated by A. V. Miller. Oxford: Oxford University Press, 1977.

————. *Philosophy of Right*. Translated by T. M. Knox. London: Oxford University Press, 1967.

———. *Science of Logic*. Translated by A. V. Miller. New York: Humanities Press, 1969.

Henrich, Dieter. *Between Kant and Hegel: Lectures on German Idealism*. Cambridge, MA: Harvard University Press, 2003.

Hickman, Larry A. *John Dewey's Pragmatic Technology*. Bloomington: Indiana University Press, 1990.

———, ed. *Reading Dewey: Interpretations for a Postmodern Generation*. Bloomington: Indiana University Press, 1998.

Houlgate, Stephen, ed. *Hegel and the Arts*. Evanston, IL: Northwestern University Press, 2007.

———, ed. *Hegel and the Philosophy of Nature*. Albany: State University of New York Press, 1998.

———. *Hegel, Nietzsche and the Criticism of Metaphysics*. Cambridge: Cambridge University Press, 1986.

———. *An Introduction to Hegel: Freedom, Truth, and History*. Oxford: Blackwell, 2005.

———. *The Opening of Hegel's "Logic": From Being to Infinity*. West Lafayette, IN: Purdue University Press, 2006.

Hyppolite, Jean. *Genesis and Structure of Hegel's "Phenomenology of Spirit."* Translated by Samuel Cherniak and John Heckman. Evanston, IL: Northwestern University Press, 1974.

Inwood, M. J. *Hegel*. New York: Routledge and Kegan Paul, 1983.

Jackson, Philip W. *John Dewey and the Lessons of Art*. New Haven, CT: Yale University Press, 1998.

———. *John Dewey and the Philosopher's Task*. New York: Teachers College Press, 2002.

———. *The Practice of Teaching*. New York: Teachers College Press, 1986.

Kant, Immanuel. *Critique of Practical Reason*. New York: Cambridge University Press, 1997.

———. *Critique of Pure Reason*. Edited by Paul Guyer and Allen W. Wood. Cambridge: Cambridge University Press, 1998.

———. *Critique of the Power of Judgment*. Translated by Paul Guyer and Eric Matthews, edited by Paul Guyer. Cambridge: Cambridge University Press, 2000.

———. *Groundwork of the Metaphysics of Morals*. New York: Harper and Row, 1964.

———. *Logic*. New York: Dover, 1974.

———. *Prolegomena to Any Future Metaphysics*. Indianapolis: Bobbs-Merrill, 1950.

———. *Religion and Rational Theology*. Edited by Allen W. Wood and George di Giovanni. Cambridge: Cambridge University Press, 1996.

———. *Religion within the Limits of Reason Alone*. New York: Harper, 1960.

Kaufmann, Walter. *Critique of Religion and Philosophy*. Princeton, NJ: Princeton University Press, 1978.

———. *Hegel: A Reinterpretation*. New York: Anchor Books, 1966.

Kestenbaum, Victor. *The Grace and Severity of the Ideal: John Dewey and the Transcendent*. Chicago: University of Chicago Press, 2002.

Knowles, Dudley. *Hegel and the Philosophy of Right*. London: Routledge, 2002.

Kolakowski, Leszek. *Modernity on Endless Trial*. Chicago: University of Chicago Press, 1990.

Körner, Stephan. *Kant*. New Haven, CT: Yale University Press, 1955.

Korsgaard, Christine M. *Creating the Kingdom of Ends*. New York: Cambridge University Press, 1996.

Lauer, Quentin. *Essays in Hegelian Dialectic*. New York: Fordham University Press, 1977.

———. *Hegel's Concept of God*. Albany: State University of New York Press, 1982.

———. *Hegel's Idea of Philosophy*. New York: Fordham University Press, 1971.

———. *A Reading of Hegel's "Phenomenology of Spirit."* New York: Fordham University Press, 1993.

Levine, Barbara, ed. *Works about John Dewey: 1886–1995*. Carbondale: Southern Illinois University Press, 1996.

Löwith, Karl. *From Hegel to Nietzsche: The Revolution in Nineteenth-Century Thought*. New York: Columbia University Press, 1964.

MacIntyre, Alisdair, comp. *Hegel: A Collection of Critical Essays*. New York: Anchor Books, 1972.

Martin, Jay. *The Education of John Dewey: A Biography*. New York: Columbia University Press, 2002.

Miller, A. V., and J. N. Findlay. *Hegel's Philosophy of Nature*. Oxford: Clarendon Press, 1970.

Morgenbesser, Sidney, ed. *Dewey and His Critics*. New York: Journal of Philosophy, 1977.

Neuhouser, Frederick. *Foundations of Hegel's Social Theory*. Cambridge, MA: Harvard University Press, 2000.

Peters, R. S., ed. *John Dewey Reconsidered*. London: Routledge and Kegan Paul, 1977.

Pinkard, Terry. *German Philosophy, 1760–1860: The Legacy of Idealism*. Cambridge: Cambridge University Press, 2002.

———. *Hegel: A Biography*. Cambridge: Cambridge University Press, 2000.

———. *Hegel's Phenomenology: The Sociality of Reason*. Cambridge: Cambridge University Press, 1996.

Pippin, Robert B. *Hegel's Idealism: The Satisfactions of Self-Consciousness*. Cambridge: Cambridge University Press, 1989.

———. *Hegel's Practical Philosophy*. Cambridge: Cambridge University Press, 2008.

———. *Idealism as Modernism*. Cambridge: Cambridge University Press, 1997.

———. *Modernism as a Philosophical Problem*. Oxford: Blackwell, 1999.

Rice, David. *Reinhold Niebuhr and John Dewey: An American Odyssey*. Albany: State University of New York Press, 1993.

Rockefeller, Steven C. *John Dewey: Religious Faith and Democratic Humanism*. New York: Columbia University Press, 1991.

Roth, Robert J. *John Dewey and Self-Realization*. Englewood Cliffs, NJ: Prentice-Hall, 1962.

Russell, Bertrand. *A History of Western Philosophy*. New York: Simon and Schuster, 1945.

Ryan, Alan. *John Dewey and the High Tide of American Liberalism*. New York: W. W. Norton, 1995.

Scruton, Roger. *Kant*. New York: Oxford University Press, 1982.

Shook, John R. *Dewey's Empirical Theory of Knowledge and Reality*. Nashville, TN: Vanderbilt University Press, 2000.

Singer, Peter. *Hegel*. Oxford: Oxford University Press, 1983.

Sleeper, R. W. *The Necessity of Pragmatism*. New Haven, CT: Yale University Press, 1986.

Solomon, Robert C. *From Hegel to Existentialism*. New York: Oxford University Press, 1987.

———. *In the Spirit of Hegel*. Oxford: Oxford University Press, 1983.

Spinoza, Benedict de. *Ethics*. Translated by George Eliot, edited by Thomas Deegan. Salzburg: Institut für Anglistik und Amerikanistik, Universität Salzburg, 1981.

Taylor, Charles. *Hegel*. Cambridge: Cambridge University Press, 1975.

———. *Hegel and Modern Society*. Cambridge: Cambridge University Press, 1979.

Tiles, J. E. *Dewey*. New York: Routledge, 1988.

Tillich, Paul. *Systematic Theology*. Vol. 1. Chicago: University of Chicago Press, 1951.

———. *Systematic Theology*. Vol. 2. Chicago: University of Chicago Press, 1957.

———. *Systematic Theology*. Vol. 3. Chicago: University of Chicago Press, 1963.

Westbrook, Robert B. *John Dewey and American Democracy*. Ithaca, NY: Cornell University Press, 1991.

Westphal, Merold. *History and Truth in Hegel's Phenomenology*. Indianapolis: Indiana University Press, 1998.

Wood, Allen W. *Hegel's Ethical Thought*. Cambridge: Cambridge University Press, 1990.

———. *Kant*. Oxford: Blackwell, 2005.

———. *Kant's Ethical Thought*. Cambridge: Cambridge University Press, 1999.

Yovel, Yirmiyahu. *Dark Riddle: Hegel, Nietzsche, and the Jews*. Cambridge: Polity Press, 1998.

———. *Hegel's Preface to the "Phenomenology of Spirit."* Princeton, NJ: Princeton University Press, 2005.

Index

Jackson, Philip W., 100
John Dewey on Education: Selected Writings (Archambault), 99

Kant (Körner), 101
Kant (Scruton), 101
Kant (Wood), 101
Kant, Immanuel, 6, 13, 16, 39, 80, 82, 88, 93, 95–97, 104, 106; common sense and reason, move from, 31; depth, and complexity of thought, 25; horizontal movement, as extensional, 25; pure reason, transcendental problems of, 80; and transcendental objects, 19–20; and unconditional necessity, 81; understanding and reason, distinction between, 30; vertical/horizontal distinction, as extensional, 25; vertical movement, as intensional, 25; works of, 101–2
Kant's Life and Thought (Cassirer), 101
Kaufmann, Walter, 101, 104, 106
Kestenbaum, Victor, 100
knowledge: body of, mastering of, 43; controlling of, 53–54; controlling and receiving elements, uniting of, 53; and experts, 43; pursuit of, 13; receiving of, 53–54; taking ownership of, 18
Kolakowski, Leszek, 105
Körner, Stephan, 101
Korsgaard, Christine, 102

Lauer, Quentin, 103–4
learning: cancel phase, 34; and criticism, 35; elevate phase, 34–35; as occurring naturally, 77; preserve phase, 34–35; and "second thought," 36; stages of, 33–35; write-revise solution of, 36

Lectures on Aesthetics (Hegel), 103
Levine, Barbara, 99
Logic (Kant), 25
Löwith, Karl, 105

MacIntyre, Alasdair, 104
manners: and moral truth, 17
Martin, Jay, 99
mattering, 58; and intrinsic worth, 56; and vocation, 57
McCarthy, Lucille, 99
metaphysics, 96
modeling, 52
modernism, 105
Moore, Marianne, 71
moral education: and "character training," 17
morals: perfection, aspiring to, 62; and philosophy, 62
moral truth, 18; and manners, 17
Morgenbesser, Sidney, 99
mutual recognition, 89; human flourishing, as essential condition for, 90; and personhood, 85
"My Pedagogic Creed" (Dewey), 72–81; rhetorical overkill of, 79–80

negation: concept of, 26; of negation, 32; in speculative thought, 32
Nietzsche, Friedrich, 104
1984 (Orwell): "double-talk" in, 79

objects of ultimate concern: as spiritual, 40
The Odyssey of Spirit (Harris), 103
On Art, Religion, and the History of Philosophy: Introductory Lectures (Hegel), 103
The Opening of Hegel's "Logic" (Houlgate), 103
Orwell, George, 79